PROBLEMS AND PERSPECTIVES IN HISTORY
EDITOR: H. F. KEARNEY M A, PH D

Origins of the Industrial Revolution

PROBLEMS AND PERSPECTIVES IN HISTORY

EDITOR: H.F. KEARNEY M A, P H D

Origins of the
Industrial Revolution

M.W. Flinn MA D.Litt

READER IN ECONOMIC HISTORY IN THE
UNIVERSITY OF EDINBURGH

LONGMAN

LONGMAN GROUP LIMITED
London
*Associated companies, branches and representatives
throughout the world*

© M.W. Flinn 1966

*First published 1966
Fifth impression 1974*

ISBN 0 582 31350 3

98514
330.942 FLIN

*Printed in Hong Kong by
Yu Luen Offset Printing Factory Ltd.*

Editor's Foreword

'Study problems in preference to periods' was the excellent advice given by Lord Acton in his inaugural lecture at Cambridge. To accept it is one thing, to put it into practice is another. In fact, in both schools and universities the teaching of history, in depth, is often hindered by certain difficulties of a technical nature, chiefly to do with the availability of sources. In this respect, history tends to be badly off in comparison with literature or the sciences. The historical equivalents of set texts, readings or experiments, in which the student is encouraged to use his own mind, are the so-called 'special periods'. If these are to be fruitful, the student must be encouraged to deal in his own way with the problems raised by historical documents and the historiography of the issues in question and he must be made aware of the wider perspectives of history. Thus, if the enclosure movement of the sixteenth century is studied, the student might examine the historiographical explanations stretching from More's *Utopia* and Cobbett to Beresford's *Lost Villages of England*. At the same time he might also be dealing with selected documents raising important problems. Finally he might be encouraged to realize the problems of peasantries at other periods of time, including Russia and China in the nineteenth and twentieth centuries. In this particular instance, thanks to Tawney and Power, *Tudor Economic Documents*, the history teacher is comparatively well off. For other special periods the situation is much more difficult. If, however, the study of history is to encourage the development of the critical faculties as well as the memory, this approach offers the best hope. The object of this series is to go some way towards meeting these difficulties.

The general plan of each volume in the series will be similar, with a threefold approach from aspects of historiography, documents and editorial consideration of wider issues, though the structure and balance between the three aspects may vary.

A broad view is being taken of the limits of history. Political history will not be excluded, but a good deal of emphasis will be placed on economic, intellectual and social history. The idea has in fact grown out of the experience of a group of historians at the University of Sussex, where the student is encouraged to investigate the frontier areas between his own and related disciplines.

H. KEARNEY

Contents

Acknowledgements

We are indebted to the following for permission to reproduce copyright material:

George Allen & Unwin Ltd for an extract from *Factors in Economic Development* by A. K. Cairncross; American Economic Association for extracts from *American Economic Review*, XLIV, No. 1, 1959, XLVI, Papers and Proceedings (1956), XLIX, Papers and Proceedings (1959), and LIII, Papers and Proceedings (1963); Mr K. E. Berrill for extracts from *Essays in the Economic and Social History of Tudor and Stuart England* ed. F. J. Fisher; Cambridge University Press for extracts from *British Economic Growth 1688–1959* by Phyllis Deane and W. A. Cole, and *Aspects of the Rise of Economic Individualism* by H. M. Robertson; Jonathan Cape Ltd and The Macmillan Company of New York for an extract from *The Industrial Revolution in the Eighteenth Century* by P. Mantoux; Frank Cass & Company Ltd for an extract from *The Industrial Revolution* by H. L. Beales; The University of Chicago Press for an extract from an article by Phyllis Deane in *Economic Development and Cultural Change*, IV, 1955–6; The Dorsey Press for extracts from *On the Theory of Social Change* by Everett E. Hagen, published in London by Tavistock Publications (1959) Ltd; the Editors of the *Economic History Review* for extracts from an article by Professor R. Davis in *Economic History Review*, Second Series, Volume XV, No. 2; Harvard University Press for an extract from *The Theory of Economic Development* by J. A. Schumpeter, Copyright 1934 and 1962 by the President and Fellows of Harvard College and Redvers Opie, and for extracts from *Economic Growth in France and Britain, 1851–1950* by Charles P. Kindleberger, Copyright 1964 by the President and Fellows of Harvard College; Heinemann Educational Books Ltd and Aktiebolaget Svenska Bokförlaget, Sweden, for extracts from *Religion and Economic Action* by K. Samuelsson, trans. E. G. French; Istanbul University for extracts from *Lectures on Economic Development* by H. J. Habakkuk and others; University of Louvain for an extract from an article by H. J. Habakkuk in *Le Progrès Economique*, 1955, ed. L. Dupriez; Macmillan & Co. Ltd for an extract from *Studies in Economic History* by G. Unwin, ed. R. H. Tawney; Macmillan & Co. Ltd, St Martin's Press, Inc. and The Macmillan Company of

ACKNOWLEDGEMENTS

Canada Ltd for extracts from *The Sources of Invention* by J. Jewkes, D. Sawers and R. Stillerman, and *The Economics of Take-Off Into Sustained Growth* by W. W. Rostow; John Murray (Publishers) Ltd for an extract from *The Royal Society of Arts 1754–1954* by D. Hudson and K. W. Luckhurst; John Murray (Publishers) Ltd and Harcourt, Brace & World, Inc. for extracts from *Religion and the Rise of Capitalism* by R. H. Tawney; Oxford University Press for extracts from *The Industrial Revolution 1760–1830* by T. S. Ashton (Home University Library 204); the Population Investigation Committee, London School of Economics for an extract from an article by A. J. Youngson in *Population Studies XV*, No. 2, November 1961; and Routledge & Kegan Paul Ltd for an extract from *English Landed Society in the Eighteenth Century* by G. E. Mingay.

I
The Industrial Revolution

When economic historians first turned their attention to the Industrial Revolution, it was a concern for the social consequences of this great upheaval which shaped their conception of it. This was natural enough for a generation brought up in the later decades of the nineteenth century for whom the urban squalor, poverty and insecurity which characterized the immediate post-Industrial Revolution era were still very much of a reality. With a zeal burnished by a vivid awareness of social injustice, Toynbee (1884), Thorold Rogers (1884) and the Hammonds (1912, 1918, 1919) all directed the shafts of their research in selected directions only, and in the process over-simplified and distorted the social and economic sequence of cause and effect.

Not unexpectedly, this biased, if humanitarian, approach ultimately provoked a reaction, and the efforts of the second generation of historians of the Industrial Revolution were directed primarily towards rectifying the imbalance of their predecessors. Clapham (1926–38), Redford (1931) and Ashton (1948), besides adding enormously to the depth of our understanding of this period, all took a much broader view of the course of events, pointing to many particular directions in which permanent benefit accrued from the economic changes.

In insisting on the importance of integrating the study of social change with that of economic development, the early economic historians were probably reacting, in part at least, from the remorseless, and – as they considered – inhumane, logic of classical political economy. This propensity to keep a weather eye cocked in the direction of current professional economic thinking has, of course, been a characteristic – and a very desirable one – of economic historians ever since. It is not surprising, therefore, that, in the interwar and immediate postwar periods, when economists necessarily focused their studies on short-term fluctuations and trade cycle theory, economic historians naturally and fruitfully projected this cyclical approach to their study of earlier periods. So far as Industrial Revolution studies were concerned, this preoccupation with the trade cycle bore rich fruit in works of the first importance by an American team, Gayer, Rostow and Schwartz (1953), and by Ashton (1959).

In contrast, the focus of the economic history of the 1950s and '60s, reflecting the switch of theoretical studies from short-run to long-run movements, has shifted sharply towards the study of economic development in its historical context. And, as in the previous phases of economic historical studies theoretical ideas proved to be invaluable tools for historical analysis, so in this new phase the economist has remained the economic historian's closest ally. Indeed, theories of economic development have burgeoned so profusely in the twenty years since the Second World War that the economic historian, laboriously filling in the bricks and mortar between the framework of the economist's theories, tends to pant along considerably in the rear of the theoretical advances. But if the economic historian, whether through lack of training or inclination, has been slow to avail himself of the conceptual and analytical tools being created in such abundance by the theorists of economic development, his laboured, and at times inexpert, quest for the touchstones of economic growth in the past has thrown a new and revealing light into some old corners of economic history. Few major fields of study have benefited more from this new approach than the Industrial Revolution.

Under the impact of these varying approaches, the conception of the Industrial Revolution has, not surprisingly, undergone some astonishing metamorphoses. At one time it has, with cataclysmic suddenness, transformed the economy overnight from feudal backwardness to the machine age: at another, it has been tamed to a movement of gradual evolution to which the very description 'revolution' appears utterly inappropriate. It has been pushed, chronologically, from pillar to post to such an extent that every fresh writer on the subject must define and defend his own choice of dates. It has been over-dramatized by emotional concentration on the 'dark, Satanic mills' (misconstruing, in the process, Blake's reference to philosophical processes), or reduced to nothingness by the discovery that there was nothing statistically remarkable about the measurable economic trends of the period. Though the proponents of these rival approaches have been stimulated by the belief that their predecessors were mistaken in their emphasis, their varied interpretations are, of course, complementary rather than mutually exclusive. The Industrial Revolution was not a particular kind of economic or social change; it was all kinds.

The cataclysmic view of the early historians was most urgently conveyed by Beard:

England of the first part of the eighteenth century was virtually a mediaeval England, quiet, primeval, and undisturbed by the roar of trade and commerce. Suddenly, almost like a thunderbolt from a clear sky, were ushered in the storm and stress of the Industrial Revolution. (Beard, 1901, 23)

Though this dramatic interpretation of the Industrial Revolution died hard, a more reasonable and moderate view commonly prevailed. Since the earlier historians were primarily concerned to explain the evolution of nineteenth-century industrial society, their tendency was to look upon the Industrial Revolution as an organ of social change. The view that the method of production determines the nature of social organization was, of course, most vigorously argued by Marx. This belief in the essentially social nature of the Industrial Revolution is perhaps best summed up by Beales:

The industrial revolution replaced one social system or one civilization by another. Before it emerged, agriculture provided the economic basis of English life: after it, the basis was industry, extractive and manufacturing. A small population became large: a narrow material equipment was expanded: low standards of consumption were made more lavish: the working classes became articulate. A civilization based on the plough and the pasture perished – in its place stood a new order, resting, perhaps dangerously, on coal, iron and imported textile materials. (Beales, 1928, 30)

The search for the kind of productive changes that were capable of imposing so radical a social revolution quickly revealed the breadth and complexity of the economic forces at work. Toynbee categorized the principal areas in which these forces operated:

The essence of the Industrial Revolution is the substitution of competition for the mediaeval regulations which had previously controlled the production and distribution of wealth. . . . Coming to the facts of the Industrial Revolution, the first thing that strikes us is the far greater rapidity which marks the growth of population. . . . Next we notice the relative and positive decline in the agricultural population. . . . Passing to manufactures, we find here the all-prominent fact to be the substitution of the factory for the domestic system, the consequence of the mechanical discoveries of the time. (Toynbee, 1884, 85–90)

3

Toynbee, therefore, gave pride of place to the coming of *laissez-faire*. Since his age was also the age of T. H. Green and the Fabian Society, it is not perhaps surprising to find *laissez-faire* the villain of the piece. Other writers (e.g. Cunningham, 1882), similarly mesmerized by the coincidence in time between the publication of the *Wealth of Nations* and Watt's improvement of the steam engine, also saw the switch from a mercantilist policy of regulation to *laissez-faire* as the key to the Industrial Revolution.

In Toynbee's interpretation this intellectual driving force was nicely balanced by the role of technology, for the central element in these early interpretations of the Industrial Revolution was invention. Seven or eight inventions, familiar to every schoolboy, set in motion the wheels of economic and social change: and since these inventions almost all fell within the first twenty-five years of the reign of George III, this fixed the starting-point of the Industrial Revolution firmly in the year 1760. The close association between industrial and agricultural change pointed inevitably to the chronology of the enclosure movement as an additional element in this interpretation. The progress of enclosure was measured by the annual number of parliamentary enclosure acts (there was little or no awareness at this stage that, in the days before enclosure by private act, a great deal of enclosure was accomplished by agreement registered in the Courts of Chancery and Exchequer). These enclosure acts showed a gratifying upward turn in the 1760s.

While British historians were still preoccupied in filling in the details of this over-simplified and over-dramatized picture, a French scholar, Mantoux, as early as 1906, produced a far more profound study of the process of economic development in Britain in the eighteenth century. His detailed examination of the agricultural, commercial and industrial changes during the whole of the century convinced him that, 'in spite of the apparent rapidity of its development, the industrial revolution sprang from far-distant causes' (Mantoux, 1928, 25). This view was echoed a few years later by Ashley (1914, 141), who observed that 'it is perhaps more important to view the development in the reign of George III as a culmination of movements already on foot than as creating something entirely new'.

This suggestion that the Industrial Revolution was not a sudden visitation on a quasi-medieval economy but the logical outcome of pre-existing strands of development carried, of course, important implications for the analysis of causes. For the time being, however, these implications were not followed up, but further reflections on the idea of gradual evolution began to sow seeds of doubt even as to the aptness of the word 'revolution' at all in this context:

> When, on looking back [wrote Unwin], we find that the revolution has been going on for two centuries, and had been in preparation for two centuries before that, when we find that both in its causes and consequences it affects the lot of that three-quarters of the human race who are still farmers and peasants as profoundly as it does that of the industrial worker, we may begin to doubt whether the term . . . has not by this time served its turn. (Unwin, 1927, 15)

Or, as another historian of the same period expressed it: 'A revolution which continued for 150 years and had been in preparation for at least another 150 years may well seem to need a new label' (Heaton, 1932, 5).

Whereas for the early historians, interested primarily in the origins of nineteenth-century society, it was largely a question of how far back it was necessary to go into the eighteenth century to find the birth of the new society, the focus of Industrial Revolution studies was now switched to the body of the eighteenth century. The appearance in 1928 of the English translation of Mantoux's now twenty-year-old study was a reminder that the most thorough and perceptive of the early historians saw the Industrial Revolution as fundamentally an eighteenth-century phenomenon:

> We have preferred, for reasons which seem to us conclusive, to close with the first years of the nineteenth century. By then the great technical inventions, including the most important invention of all, the steam engine, had all become practical realities. Many factories were already at work which, apart from certain details as to tools, were identical with those of today. Great centres of industry had begun to grow up, a factory proletariat made its appearance, the old trade regulations, already more than half destroyed, made way for the system of *laissez-faire*, itself even then doomed through the pressure of already half-perceived necessities. The law which inaugurated factory legislation was passed in 1802. The stage was ready set; there was nothing left but to follow the working out of the drama. (Mantoux, 1928, 43)

The 1920s and '30s saw the publication of a number of studies of individual major industries and industrial regions in the eighteenth century (Ashton, 1924; Ashton and Sykes, 1929; Court, 1938; Dickinson, 1938; Dodd, 1933; Heaton, 1920; Wadsworth and Mann, 1931) which, though not attempting in any way to conceal the sharp change in both the level of output and the method of organization which occurred in many, though not all, of these industries, established much more firmly the continuity of eighteenth-century industrial history. Much has been read into the complete omission of any reference to the term *industrial revolution* in Sir John Clapham's monumental study of the *Economic History of Modern Britain* (1926–38), but whether this was intentional or not, there was a certain justification for this in a book dealing with the period from 1820. More significant, probably, was a similar virtual exclusion of the expression from Redford's study of the classic period of the Industrial Revolution of 1931.

In the postwar period, the first historian to attempt a synthesis of the cataclysmic and evolutionary interpretations was Ashton (1948). His Industrial Revolution was broadly set within the context of society as a whole. 'The changes were not merely "industrial",' he wrote, 'but also social and intellectual.' In addition to the familiar developments in industry, agriculture and transport, his net drew in changes in the age structure of the population, the supply of capital, the influence of both short- and long-term variations in the level of the public debt, the supply and characteristic quality of entrepreneurs, the nature of the process of invention, the quickening of the pace of advance in pure science, and the extent and nature of educational services.

Out of this broad conspectus it is possible to select two themes which struck a particular chord in Ashton's imagination, and which, though never allowed to usurp a disproportionate status in his analysis, may nevertheless be said to occupy central positions in his characterization of the Industrial Revolution. The first of these concerned the role of Dissent:

It has often been observed that the growth of industry was connected historically with the rise of groups which dissented from the
Church by law established in England. . . . Many explanations have
been offered of this close association between industry and Dissent.
It has been suggested that those who sought out new forms of worship would also naturally strike out new paths in secular fields. It has
been argued that there is an intimate connexion between the tenets
peculiar to Nonconformity and the rules of conduct that lead to
success in business. And it has been asserted that the exclusion of
Dissenters from the universities, and from office in government and
administration, forced many to seek an outlet for their abilities in

6

industry and trade. There may be something in each of these contentions, but a simpler explanation lies in the fact that, broadly speaking, the Nonconformists constituted the better educated section of the middle classes. (Ashton, 1948, 17–19)

Both in this study of the Industrial Revolution and in his later, larger work on the eighteenth-century economy (Ashton, 1953), Ashton has found space for many affectionate references to Quaker iron-masters, Unitarian cotton-spinners and Presbyterian engineers. He was primarily concerned with the role of Dissent in industry as a characteristic feature of the Industrial Revolution, and avoided entering into any deeper discussion of the controversial issue of the causal connection between religious change and economic development. Nonetheless, in stressing the apparently disproportionate share of dissenters in the field of industrial management and innovation, Ashton opened the way to a possible element in the explanation of the origins of the Industrial Revolution.

Ashton's second major theme was the function of the rate of interest in stimulating economic expansion:

The importance of the lowering of the rate of interest in the half-century before the industrial revolution has never been properly stressed by historians. If we seek – it would be wrong to do so – for a single reason why the pace of economic development quickened about the middle of the eighteenth century, it is to this we must look. (Ashton, 1948, 11)

For the first time in the study of the Industrial Revolution, the practised eye of the economist was beginning to stress some key aspects of the mechanism of economic growth that had hitherto escaped the attention of historians viewing the Industrial Revolution primarily as a techno-logical and social phenomenon. Indeed, if one were to attempt to summarize Ashton's contribution to the study of the Industrial Revo-lution in a single sentence, it would probably be best expressed in terms of his approaching the subject from the standpoint of an economist. In doing so he introduced into historical generalization an element of economic analysis hitherto largely lacking and set a course from which the study of the Industrial Revolution has subsequently benefited enormously.

The analytical approach was taken a stage further by the American economist, Rostow (1960). Rostow's systematization of the process of economic growth was intended, of course, to be a general model, and it is in this light that his theory has excited most discussion. Nevertheless, his theory draws heavily on the British experience, and, though it has been criticized for failing to measure up exactly to the facts of British history, has nevertheless done much to focus attention on the mechanism of growth in the British Industrial Revolution.

Briefly, Rostow simplified the process of economic growth for analytical purposes by distinguishing five 'stages' of growth. Of these five stages – 'the traditional society', 'the preconditions for take-off', 'the take-off', 'the drive to maturity' and 'the age of high mass-consumption' – only the second and third are immediately relevant to the subject of this book. Pursuing the analogy of an aeroplane taking off from the ground, Rostow's 'take-off into self-sustained growth' (the fuller phrase, used when Rostow first introduced the concept (1956), was abbreviated in later writings) implied that a certain rate of growth will maintain itself – just as an aircraft, having gained sufficient speed to get it off the ground, can, if it maintains that speed, keep flying. 'Growth becomes [the economy's] normal condition. Compound interest becomes built, as it were, into its habits and institutional structure' (Rostow, 1960, 7).

The take-off is defined 'as requiring all three of the following related conditions:

1. a rise in the rate of productive investment from, say, 5 per cent or less to over 10 per cent of national income;

2. the development of one or more substantial manufacturing sectors, with a high rate of growth;

3. the existence or quick emergence of a political, social and institutional framework which exploits the impulses to expansion in the modern sector' (Rostow, 1960, 39).

The last of these is so vague that it would be extremely difficult to determine whether or not the necessary conditions existed in a growing economy. The second, relating to what Rostow has called elsewhere 'leading sectors', represents a particularly useful addition to the armoury of analytical weapons. 'The effects of a sector touched by new technology and experiencing a rapid growth phase transcend the sector itself.' Rostow distinguished three directions in which the stimulus of a rapidly-expanding leading sector ramifies through the economy.

Backward Effects. Depending on its technological character, the new sector, in its rapid growth phase, will set up requirements for new inputs of raw materials and machinery which require, in turn, an extension of modern contriving attitudes and methods. . . .

Lateral Effects. In addition, the leading sector will induce around it a whole set of changes which tend to reinforce the industrialization process on a wider front. Modern industrial activity surrounded itself with urban men, services, and institutions whose existence strengthened the foundations for industrialization as an ongoing process: a disciplined working force organized around the hierarchies decreed by technique; professional men to handle the problems of law and relations to the various markets for input and products; urban overhead capital; institutions of banking and commerce; and the construction and service industries required to meet the needs of those who manned the new industrial structure. . . .

Forward Effects. Finally, modern industrial activity created the setting in which new industrial activity was induced, either by cutting the cost of an input to another industry; by providing a new product or service whose existence was a challenge to the enterprising to exploit; or by creating a bottleneck whose removal was evidently profitable and which therefore attracted inventive talent and entrepreneurship. Leading sectors thus set up incentives and open up possibilities for a wide range of new economic activities, sometimes, even, setting the stage for the next major leading sector. (Rostow, 1963, 4–6)

Rarely can a leading sector maintain its growth for long: deceleration soon sets in, and the continued growth of the economy as a whole depends upon new leading sectors emerging to take over as the initial impetus of the preceding one begins to wane. Most, if not all, of the multiplier effects suggested by Rostow may be traced in the successive development of canals, the cotton industry, the iron industry, the engineering industry and railway construction in Britain in the period beginning about 1760.

Rostow's third requirement for the take-off relates to the rate of net investment. By suggesting that the key determinant of the take-off is the achievement of a net investment rate of 10 per cent of the net national product, he introduced a very precise statistical criterion. Not only is it not possible to arrive at any very exact measurement of income and investment in economies as statistically primitive as Britain in the eighteenth century, but, as Habakkuk and Deane have argued:

It is difficult to credit that a change of this order of magnitude could have occurred in Britain in the last two decades of the eighteenth century. . . . The quantitative data for the period – for what they are worth – do not support a shift of this order of magnitude. (Habakkuk and Deane, 1963, 75)

This is probably true, but the quantitative data are both imperfect and extremely incomplete, and it is conceivable that the rather limited range of investment considered by Habakkuk and Deane offers an insufficiently reliable guide to the trend of investment generally. Possibly, too, Rostow's insistence on a 10 per cent minimum exceeds what is, in practice, necessary to sustain moderately rapid growth. Even lacking the necessary statistics, what is known of investment activity in the various sectors of the economy – industry, agriculture, transport, urban building and other social overheads – indicates beyond doubt *some* increase in the rate of net investment in the late eighteenth century, and it is possible that the extent of this increase was sufficient to sustain rapid growth. (Hughes, 1964, 71–2)

Rostow's scheme has been criticized on the grounds that economic development lacks the scientific orderliness of biological growth; that if the stages are merely 'ages' or chronological phases they tend to become arbitrary divisions; that, while it describes some aspects of economic development, 'it fails to specify any mechanism of evolution which links the different stages'; that economic development does not always follow his sequence of stages, abortive take-offs being possible, as well as the telescoping of stages; that the discontinuity implicit in the division of growth into stages turns out on closer examination to be no more than a simple acceleration of growth; that, in particular, there are many elements of overlap or confusion between the stages of 'pre-conditions' and 'take-off' (Cairncross, 1961; Baran and Hobsbawm, 1961).

Nevertheless, when all this and much more has been said, and when it is recalled that Rostow has been seeking, in conscious imitation of Marx (*The Stages of Economic Growth* – is subtitled 'A Non-Communist Manifesto'), to systematize the process of growth generally and not merely for the single example of the British experience, it remains evident that Rostow has left a permanent imprint upon the Industrial Revolution. In the post-Rostovian period the attention of historians is focused upon rates of growth and investment, upon the multiplier effects of growth in individual sectors and, in general terms, upon the mechanism of acceleration. Most important of all, Rostow drew attention to qualitative developments at different phases of growth. Even if growth, as Cairncross suggests, is not discontinuous, there must be a priority, an order, in different types of changes and investment.

Following closely upon the heels of this analytical advance, a recent major study by Deane and Cole (1962) has widened horizons still further. Their method was to assemble every available statistic relating to economic development (to which they added a number of carefully considered estimates), and to draw such conclusions concerning economic growth as strict statistical fact permitted. So far as the eighteenth century is concerned, the greatest quantity of statistics available relates to trade and population, and Deane and Cole have accordingly pursued their most detailed analysis in these directions. The course of development of some industries may be inferred from imports of raw materials, or, less satisfactorily, occasionally from exports. For the national product, agricultural output, and the output of most industries, they have had to rely upon contemporary estimates which they have subjected to intensive scrutiny and, from time to time, amended.

So far as overall growth is concerned, they found that there is

little evidence of growth in the first four decades of the century, but beginning in the 1740s there was a marked upward trend in absolute totals though little improvement in the rate of growth in incomes per head until the last two or three decades. A considerably sharper upward trend appears in the 1780s and 1790s. . . . Real national output is estimated to have grown at about 0·3 per cent per annum over the period before 1745, 0·9 per cent over 1745–85, and 1·8 per cent over the last two decades of the century. The corresponding rates of growth in output per head were 0·3, 0·3 and 0·9 per cent. (Deane and Cole, 1962, 280)

It is the upturn of the rate of growth in the 1740s which constitutes their most original contribution to eighteenth-century studies. For them, the faster rate of growth they discern after 1745 is, in a way, more decisive than the second acceleration of the classic period of the take-off.

The beginnings of sustained economic growth can be traced to the middle of the eighteenth century when the overall rate of growth seems to have risen to near 1 per cent per annum from probably not more than about 0·3 per cent per annum. At this stage, however, the expansion of the economy was apparently swamped by the growth of population which also dates from slightly before mid-century. (Deane and Cole, 1962, 285)

Or, as Habakkuk and Deane (1963, 82) expressed it, 'the sustained rise in the rate of growth in total output probably dates back to the 1740s'.

The evidence for this turning-point in the 1740s derives largely from the overseas trade figures, from estimates of the output of a number of industries (themselves drawn from imports of raw materials or from excise returns) or from estimated average consumption figures multiplied by estimated population. The higher production was not based extensively on any new methods of production, and it is explained in terms of 'the wage-earning population as a whole [working] harder to maintain their traditional standard of life' (Deane and Cole, 1962, 93).

Total output, according to this analysis, continued to grow in the third quarter of the eighteenth century, though at a reduced pace; but since more rapid population growth had now got under way, average real output, in fact, remained stationary. The first stages of a Malthusian impasse seemed to have been reached. However, in the last quarter of the century the expansion of total output eventually outpaced population, and growth in real terms was resumed. Even now, the growth was modest – 2 per cent per annum for total real output, and barely 1 per cent for real output per head.

Seen in terms of output in this way, the economic expansion of the eighteenth century was not particularly impressive. It was a two-phase affair in which periods of moderate growth in the two middle decades and the last quarter of the century were matched by periods of slower growth in the first four decades and the third quarter of the century.

Deane and Cole are the first to admit, in some instances, the extreme unreliability of their statistical sources; but, in the words of one critic,

> one feature of the general approach to evidence in Deane and Cole that is endlessly frustrating is the tendency to advance a most tentative hypothesis, to go on at length about the inadequacies of the data, and then slowly to turn hypothesis into hard fact without relevant supporting evidence. (Hughes, 1964, 79)

The population statistics, for example, based as they are on the extremely unreliable parish register returns, may turn out not to provide a sufficiently reliable basis for generalizations about short- or medium-run trends in *per capita* output. The extent and general significance of the acceleration of growth in the 1740s have not yet been fully assessed, and since the growth does not appear to have been sustained during the next quarter-century, it may turn out to be little more than the kind of economic spurt that is known to have occurred in earlier centuries, say in the 1540s, without signifying a turning-point of the decisive and unmistakable nature of that of the last two decades of the eighteenth century.

Nevertheless, the statistical approach has added a new dimension of immense value to the study of the Industrial Revolution in Britain. It has allowed hypotheses to be checked against fact, brought to light many significant developments which had hitherto escaped notice and contributed enormously to the important task of historical perspective. But so far as the eighteenth century is concerned, it is subject to two serious dangers. The first arises from the apparent finality of statistics. A figure appears to be a fact, and a conclusion logically and accurately drawn from such figures appears unchallengeable. While this happy situation may be true of many twentieth-century economic statistics, it is unfortunately very seldom true of eighteenth-century statistics. None of the available figures relating to eighteenth-century economic development is wholly reliable, and some of them are devastatingly mis-leading. Trade figures cannot take smuggling into account (though Deane and Cole make allowances from time to time for fluctuations in smuggling activity); excise returns suffer from similar evasions; population figures reflect only registered baptisms and burials, not actual births and deaths; and most other 'statistics' are merely some-body's estimates. There are seldom exactly the official series which the economic historian wants today, and to supply his need he is driven to adapting related series, a process which inevitably introduces a second-ary set of errors. In the study of eighteenth-century economic history, it is seldom safe to accept a generalization based on figures alone, unless it can be supported by some confirmatory, non-quantitative evidence.

The second danger is more fundamental to the study of the Industrial Revolution. This is simply that, in the enthusiasm for quantification, the non-measurable factors get pushed into the background or are for-gotten completely. Thus, while it is no criticism of Deane and Cole that they base their interpretation of the economic development of the eighteenth century almost wholly on what is measurable (they were never attempting to do more than offer a commentary on a collection of historical statistics), their very conscious concentration on statistical evidence leads them to stress as a turning-point in history a period which seems to have little significance in other than statistical terms. The last two decades of the eighteenth century may, in a purely statistical sense, be merely an extrapolation of a curve already beginning to rise in the 1740s, but, in contrast to the developments of the 1740s and '50s, those of the 1780s and '90s were accompanied by such a plethora of non-measurable but often revolutionary changes concerned with methods of production, social institutions and the growth of towns that, in the broadest historical perspective, the relatively slight upward shifts in output and trade in the former period were dwarfed by the over-whelming transformation of society initiated in the latter.

The several generations of historians who have studied the Industrial Revolution since the pioneering days of Cunningham, Toynbee and Thorold Rogers have each reflected, as is the habit of historians, the particular point of view of their ages. Because they were describing not an event but an epoch, their conceptions have varied as widely as their viewpoints. And just as each generation has benefited, as it has differed, from its predecessor, so the present generation, while it may pride itself on yet another fresh approach, would be unwise to sweep aside the earlier interpretations too hastily. Each of the varied approaches has something to contribute: the interpretations from Toynbee to the present day are mutually complementary, adding breadth, depth and colour to the original conception. For the present generation of scholars the Industrial Revolution is a much more complex movement than it was, say, for the nineteenth-century historians, for it embodies the cumulative wisdom of several schools of thought.

Of the varying approaches, those with a quantitative basis seem, in spite of their shortcomings, to offer the firmest foundation. Most of the aggregate series at present available agree in showing significant acceleration in the rate of growth in the last two decades of the century. They also tend to confirm what a number of industrial historians have already demonstrated from literary sources – that there was a long history of moderate expansion throughout most of the first three-quarters of the century. The acceleration in the aggregate rate of growth that occurred in the last quarter of the century is, of course, a compound of moderate growth in some sectors and dramatic expansion in others. The latter comprise what every schoolboy knows of the Industrial Revolution – the cotton industry, the manufacture and utilization of steam engines, the iron industry and canal construction.

The chronology of growth in these highly dynamic sectors is fairly clear. The cotton industry (as distinct from the steadily growing fustian and linen industries which gave it birth) sprang into existence overnight with the first powered spinning mills of the early 1770s: its growth was extremely rapid after 1780. The coke iron industry may be said to have begun to emerge in the later 1750s: its progress was relatively slow until the 1780s, when the possibilities of Cort's puddling and rolling processes encouraged an enormous acceleration of growth. While there had been a steady trade in Newcomen steam pumps for mine drainage throughout the first three-quarters of the century, the adaptation of Watt's engine to rotary motion in 1781 was the really significant date in the utilization of steam power. The application of rotary motion to the blast furnace, to textile machinery and to other forms of industrial production was the true beginning of the new industrial era. The first canals were planned in the 1750s: the rate of canal construction accelerated in the 1770s and reached its peak in the 1790s. The major acceleration in all these sectors is heavily concentrated in the last quarter of the century: there was little expansion in any of them before 1770, and in none was there any activity at all before 1755. If there were the beginnings of faster economic growth in the economy as a whole in the 1740s, they could have had little direct connection with the sectors whose growth constituted the central feature of the Industrial Revolution.

Beside these sectors of rapid growth there were others of substantial, if slower, expansion. These – which include coalmining, the textiles other than cotton (wool, linen and silk), copper, lead, chemicals, glass, paper, building and agriculture – showed some acceleration of growth towards the end of the century, but not of the order of the more dynamic sectors. Had it not been for the former explosive group of fast-growing industries, it is likely that the moderate growth which had characterized the economy for most of the first three-quarters of the eighteenth century would have been comfortably sustained. Thus, the lesson to be learnt from the statistics appears to be one of the superimposition upon a steadily growing economy of a small group of extremely dynamic sectors. Statistically these represented, even by the end of the century, a very small share of the national product; but the growth in them was sufficient to double the existing rate of overall growth in the economy.

The increased rate of growth was sustained because radical alterations were made to the organization of both production and society which materially shifted the balance between different ways of life. If agricultural labour was still the largest occupational group at the beginning of the nineteenth century, it was not going to remain so for long: the urban industrial way of life was rapidly increasing its following. This was the area of change which first attracted historians to the Industrial Revolution, and which, in the flurry of enthusiasm for statistical investigation, sometimes gets overlooked nowadays. The back-to-back rows of Leeds, the teeming tenements of Glasgow, the crowded courts of Manchester and the sprawling cancer of the coalfields were the means by which the economic fact of growth was translated into the reality of human environment. Factories the size of New Lanark, with its two thousand workers, may have been few in number, but those with a hundred or two were becoming numerous. Textile factories, large or small, were new, and they brought with them the myriad problems of social adjustment brilliantly analysed by Neil Smelser (1959). Trade unions on anything other than an ephemeral, local scale; radical agitation for class ends rather than bread; and the futile war of man against machine make little showing on a statistical reckoning of economic change, but they, too, were an integral part of this great social transformation.

Something had happened to ways of life to change men's attitudes. Nor was it merely the attitudes of the mass of the working people, rural as well as urban, that changed: the commercial and landed classes, too, showed a livelier attitude to novelty which was part a response to and part cause of the quickened pace of change. The Industrial Revolution with which this book is concerned is therefore a more profound movement than a mere acceleration in the rate of growth of investment or national product. The higher levels of production were achieved by new technologies that demanded innovations in the organization of production. These, in turn, shifted the physical distribution of population and altered the pattern of social relationships between worker and employer as well as between the workers themselves. The economic and geographical changes, in other words, were accompanied by social and cultural changes no less dramatic or fundamental.

Though most of these social and cultural changes sprang from the basic fact of the acceleration in the rate of economic growth, the process of transformation was infinitely more complex than such a simple linkage of cause and effect would suggest. Population growth, urbanization, the advance of technology, social attitudes themselves – all were interlinked inextricably in the process of growth.

The more complex the process to be explained, the more complex the explanation. Yet, oddly enough, in spite of the constant reshaping under the influence of successive historical approaches of the character of the Industrial Revolution, its origins have scarcely interested historians at all until very recently. This may reflect no more than a due sense of priorities: until the nature of the revolution was established, exploration of its origins was unlikely to be rewarding. Until the postwar generation, the Industrial Revolution was a fact which was customarily accepted, and if its causes were considered at all, they were dismissed with a few simple generalizations about inventions or colonial trade. Looking at the Industrial Revolution from back to front, starting, that is, with results instead of causes, the early studies were little concerned with first causes. By the time they had traced the origins of this new industrial civilization to a handful of new processes, to a new-found commercial and industrial freedom, to some thinly substantiated turns in the trends of population growth, and above all to the creative power of steam, they had enough to fill their plates. It was a conception that satisfied by its obvious logic and its chronological neatness. And the tendency of interwar historians to prefer a 'gradual' interpretation absolved them from the need to explain a dramatic transformation: the steady evolution they depicted called for a different type of analysis. Even after the Second World War, when whole battalions of economists were dissecting the mechanisms of economic growth, interest among economic historians in this aspect of the Industrial Revolution languished.

A major corner was turned in 1948, when Ashton offered an original and carefully argued hypothesis concerning the key question of the supply of capital. Moreover, since 1948 some important strides have been taken to facilitate the study of the origins of the British Industrial Revolution. The debate on the causes of the acceleration in the rate of growth of population has been reopened, after it seemed that the last word had been spoken on it in the 1920s by Griffith (1926); and the relationship between this acceleration and the initiation of more rapid industrial growth is being explored in the light of the experience of other economies and other periods about which more exact statistical knowledge is available. The publication of Mrs E. B. Schumpeter's invaluable and comprehensive statistics of English overseas trade returns for the eighteenth century (1960) has lent an exactitude to the analysis of the role of foreign and colonial markets which was hitherto lacking. Mitchell and Deane's collection of historical statistics (1962) has brought together in convenient form every other available statistic from the late seventeenth century onwards. An entirely new social dimension has very recently been introduced in the study of the

Industrial Revolution by American economists and psychologists, and, whether one agrees with the somewhat exaggerated claims made by them for the new light cast on what has hitherto been the undisputed province of economic theory, it is clear that they have driven in the thin point of a very important wedge (see Chapter V). No student of the Industrial Revolution can afford to ignore their contribution.

It is not to be expected that the study of the origins of the Industrial Revolution so recently begun should have led yet to any definitive conclusions. Nonetheless, a fairly substantial body of statistical and literary evidence is now available which is relevant to this discussion. In the following four chapters some of the principal economic and social changes which paved the way for the Industrial Revolution are examined. In the final chapter an attempt is made to bring the separate parts of the analysis together into an integrated model.

II
The Demographic Origins

Economic expansion and population growth tend to be closely associated: the former seldom occurs without the latter. Though this generalization is as true of today as it is of past centuries, nonetheless a distinction must be made between the relationship of these two aspects of growth in a twentieth-century context, and the same relationship in earlier periods. In the twentieth century, and more particularly since the Second World War, the widespread diffusion of efficient techniques of preventive and curative medicine has led to sharp reductions of death rates in underdeveloped countries that have little or no causal relationship with any economic growth which may or may not occur simultaneously. Before the twentieth century, however, even in the economically more advanced countries, there were few medical advances likely to reduce mortality substantially: in these circumstances mortality rates were more likely to fluctuate in direct response to economic stimuli. Nor was the converse relationship between population growth and economic development any more consistent or automatic. The history of Ireland in the eighteenth and nineteenth centuries is eloquent testimony to the fact that rapid economic growth is far from being a necessary or inevitable accompaniment to rapid population growth.

Thus, even though the two forms of growth have tended to occur at roughly the same periods of history, they are not *necessarily* related. But they might be; and, if they were, the relationship could take a variety of forms. The purpose of this chapter is to suggest that, in the British experience in the eighteenth century, there were some respects in which causal relationships existed; but the form these relationships took cannot easily, for various reasons, be accurately or conclusively described, and has been, as will be seen, the subject of much controversy.

The censuses of population establish the fact that the population of Britain roughly doubled in the first half of the nineteenth century. Though there is far less certainty about the magnitude of growth in earlier periods, it is unlikely that population growth exceeded 75 per cent in the whole of the sixteenth and seventeenth centuries combined.

Between the late seventeenth and early nineteenth centuries there must therefore have been some appreciable acceleration in the rate of growth of population – an acceleration from a rate of probably less than 5 per cent per decade in the seventeenth century to one of about 15 per cent per decade in the early nineteenth century. While approximate limits may therefore be set to the period within which the acceleration in the rate of growth of population began, these limits are fairly wide: without a more precise determination of the chronology of population growth in the eighteenth century, they would allow for the possibility of the acceleration of population growth occurring before, during or after the initiation of rapid economic growth.

The acceleration in the rate of economic growth was centred in the last quarter of the eighteenth century. Since the maximum rate of population growth was not achieved until the second or third decade of the nineteenth century, one possibility is that the upturn in the rate of growth of population came very late in the eighteenth century, in which case it might have been preceded by the beginnings of more rapid economic growth and therefore, possibly, have been a consequence of it. On the other hand, in view of the natural tendency for population change to be gradual in its nature, the acceleration in the rate of growth of population may have begun earlier in the eighteenth century. In this case it would more clearly have preceded the phase of accelerating economic growth, a chronology which would open the door to the possibility of a causal link between population growth and economic growth in another direction. If, as a third hypothesis, the acceleration of both population growth and economic growth occurred simultaneously in the last quarter of the eighteenth century, then the two forms of growth might be interpreted as interacting parts of a mechanism of mutual development in which the process of cause and effect would be much more difficult to disentangle.

Thus, as a first step to establishing the role of population growth in the process of economic development, the determination of the chronology of the acceleration in the rate of growth of population is of some importance. Allied closely to this requirement is a second desideratum: an understanding of the causes of the acceleration in the rate of growth of population would help in establishing the nature of the relationship between population and economic growth. Population growth occurs (or accelerated growth is promoted) as a result of either a decline in the death rate or an increase in the birth rate (or both changes occurring simultaneously). Birth or death rate changes are not likely to occur in isolation: a change in one is likely to lead to a consequential change in the other, particularly in the circumstances of eighteenth-century Britain. For example, in an age when a high proportion of the population died before reaching the age of forty-five, a reduction in the death rate would have permitted a higher proportion of women to reach or complete their child-bearing period (thus allowing birth rate to increase). Whereas only 40 per cent of the marriages of the cohort of the British peerage born in the last quarter of the seventeenth century were marriages of completed fertility (i.e. lasting until the wife's forty-fifth birthday), 63 per cent of those of the last quarter of the eighteenth century were so (Hollingsworth, 1965, 23). On the other hand, an increase in the birth rate, by increasing population without (for a few years at least) increasing the productive capacity of the labour force, and by increasing the size of the family to be maintained on a given family income, might tend temporarily to increase the death rate. Both these interconnections are subject to modification according to the exact age group in which the reduction in the death rate is concentrated. But whatever the exact form of the interaction of changes in birth and death rates, the changes themselves can be divided into primary and secondary changes – into those which are autonomous, and those which are consequential upon prior changes in another rate; and in the quest for origins it is the autonomous changes which are significant.

It is difficult to explain a significant rise in the birth rate in the pre-contraception era in other than economic terms. Apart from changes in fecundity, which, on the whole, are gradual rather than erratic, this variable depends primarily upon changes in the proportion of women who marry, and changes in the age at which women marry. Both these variables, particularly the latter, are mainly influenced in the short run by economic changes. The economic changes that appear to be most relevant to this effect are connected with wage levels, which have a direct influence on marriage rates, and changes in the structure of employment. There have always tended to be social and occupational variations in both age at marriage and marital fertility, and it is quite possible that occupations associated with relatively high fertility rates were gaining in the eighteenth century relative to those with lower rates. Marital fertility rates might also have been associated with the availability of employment for children, as well as with the nature of the social services – whether, for example, poor relief includes family allowances or not. It follows from these considerations that birth rate changes occur more commonly as *consequences* of changes in the rate of economic growth rather than as *causes*. This does not rule out the possibility of birth rate changes influencing the course of economic growth through a slightly more complex process – *some* economic growth inducing a higher birth rate which in turn leads to *greater* economic growth – but the balance of probability seems to lie with an economic causation. In either event, however, a precise chronology of birth rate changes will be helpful: the pattern of cause and effect will differ according to whether the birth rate increase occurred before, during or after the moment of acceleration of economic growth.

Changes in the death rate, on the other hand, may be explained in both economic and non-economic terms. A rise in real income might reduce death rates by raising individual food consumption (particularly effective, of course, in economies in which a large proportion of the population lives at or below subsistence level), or by increasing the funds available to public authorities for expenditure on public health services or improved housing. Even without raising income levels, changes in dietary habits or land tenure might produce a similar effect. The introduction, for example, of the potato as a foodstuff of mass-consumption in the eighteenth century may have had this effect, the potato being more generally nutritious in terms of money income spent or land cultivated than other crops (Drake, 1963, 312). On the non-economic side, the most powerful influences are, of course, medical, being dependent upon techniques of preventive and curative medicine and the extent of the provision of medical services (number of doctors, hospitals, clinics, etc.). A high proportion of all deaths in the eighteenth century resulted from infectious disease both epidemic and endemic, and, from whatever cause, there seems to have been some reduction in the incidence and severity of epidemics from the middle decades of the eighteenth century. It may be that epidemiology rather than economics may explain some of the fluctuations in mortality: 'epidemic diseases, like empires, decline and fall' (Dubos, 1953, 18). And, as with birth rate changes, the chronologies of both economic and non-economic influences on the death rate are of prime importance to the analysis of the interaction of population and economic developments. These changes, too, could occur before, during or after the moment of acceleration of economic growth, the chronological relationship being a major element in the causal explanation.

In the context of eighteenth-century Britain, these considerations amount to trying to establish the extent to which particular population changes were the *result* of economic development, or sprang from forces which were, from an economic point of view, fortuitous. ... Did the Industrial Revolution create its own labour force? Or did the vagaries of disease and the weather produce an additional population that either stimulated an Industrial Revolution or had the luck to coincide with one independently generated? (Habakkuk, 1958 (1), 488, 500)

The first requirements, then, in an analysis of the interaction of population and economic movements in eighteenth-century Britain, are some understanding of the relative roles of birth rate and death rate changes, of the timing of these changes and, if possible, of their causes. Unfortunately, the paucity or unreliability of statistical material relating to these changes in eighteenth-century Britain deny us easy access to this understanding. The first Census of Population was taken in 1801, and before that date there are only estimates made either by contemporaries or by historians. Two contemporary estimates have been accepted as reasonably reliable – that by Gregory King for England and Wales in 1695 (Gonner, 1912; Glass, 1949), and that by Alexander Webster for Scotland in 1755 (Youngson, 1961). Virtually all other estimates depend upon adjustment of the figures collected at the time of the first Census by John Rickman from the parish registers of England and Wales. These series relate to the baptisms, marriages and burials recorded in parish registers at ten-yearly intervals from 1700 to 1780, and for each year between 1781 and 1800. The problem of relating numbers of baptisms and burials to those of births and deaths involves taking account of a large number of both known and unknown defects in the registers. The problem is not so much that of the extent of the discrepancies between baptisms and births and burials and deaths, as the fact that these discrepancies varied in an indeterminable way with the passage of time. Although elaborate and painstaking attempts have been made (notably by Krause, 1958, and Deane and Cole, 1962, 99–135) to overcome these difficulties, the results are not wholly convincing, not merely because they tend to minimize the shortcomings of the material but also because the conclusions they lead to are sometimes at variance with the conclusions suggested by other non-quantitative evidence.

It is, of course, this paucity or unreliability of statistical sources which has opened the way for a range of possible, and often conflicting, explanations of the increase in the rate of growth of British population in the eighteenth century. Taking the chronology of acceleration first, the traditional view, based largely on the evidence of the parish register returns, is that 'before the Industrial Revolution began the population of England was practically stationary and conditions were changing but slowly' (Griffith, 1926, 255), and that almost all the expansion occurred after 1760 as a result of an acceleration in the rate of growth beginning only after the middle of the century. Indeed, the parish register material, which, according to the most recent evaluation (Deane and Cole, 1962, 103), shows a population for England and Wales of 5·83 million in 1701, 6·14 million in 1751 and 9·16 million in 1801 (growth rates of 5 per cent and 49 per cent for the first and second halves of the century respectively), permits of no other conclusion. Since, however, the parish register returns are subject to some degree of error (arising from the process of converting baptism and burial figures into birth and death rates, as well as into total population figures), this chronology is acceptable only to the extent that one is willing to discount the short-comings of this source. Quite a small error in the 1751 figure, for example, would significantly alter the relationship between the growth rates in the two halves of the century.

Some recent work has opened the possibility of a different chrono-logy. Taking a longer view of population movements since the Middle Ages, and employing some ingenious extrapolations, Tucker (1963, 218) has postulated 'a rate of natural increase at the beginning of the eighteenth century *already* nearly as high as that during the vital revolution itself'. Similarly, Youngson has made an instructive comparison derived from Webster's 'private' census of Scotland in 1755:

Despite some imperfections, [Webster's] *Account* was obviously thoroughly done, and done by a man of ability, uniquely placed to carry it through. It should probably be taken as referring to approximately 1750. It gives the population of Scotland as 1·265 million. The corrected census figure for Scotland in 1801 is 1·678 million, and for Great Britain the figure is 10·943 million. The usual guess for Great Britain in 1750 is about 7·25 million or 7·5 million. But if Webster's figure for Scotland is approximately correct, and if it is supposed that population grew at about the same rate in England and Wales as it seems to have done in Scotland between 1750 and 1800, then Webster's *Account* suggests a distinctly larger figure, about 8·2 million, for the population of Britain in the middle of the eighteenth century. It may be, of course, that population grew faster in England

and Wales than in Scotland during the second half of the eighteenth century. But, even making reasonable allowance for this possibility, it remains doubtful whether the population of Great Britain about 1750 should be reckoned at much less than eight million. (Youngson, 1961, 200)

These two contributions imply a more gradual acceleration than that previously assumed, and one which began earlier than the second half of the eighteenth century. The hypothesis is supported by the trends in the grain trade: the sudden falling-off in corn exports in the 1750s and their replacement by net imports in the 1760s implies either a remarkable reduction in grain production (which does not seem likely), a sharp increase in *per capita* consumption (which also does not seem likely) or a decisive increase in the number of consumers which must have already begun by the 1750s.

To push back the beginning of the acceleration in this way involves the acceptance of a second phase of acceleration in the early nineteenth century, since it is clear that the rate of growth in the first decades of the nineteenth century was appreciably higher than this hypothesis would allow for the later eighteenth century. This second acceleration would not be beyond the bounds of possibility, having regard to the introduction of vaccination at the turn of the century; but, if it did occur, it could have played no part in the initiation of the Industrial Revolution.

Further assessment of these rival chronologies may be assisted by some consideration of the underlying causes of the acceleration. This aspect of the population history of the eighteenth century has had an even more chequered history. Until quite recently the assumption that the increase in the rate of growth was due to a reduction in the death rate was not seriously challenged. Griffith's view was that the explanation lay primarily in a reduction of the death rate, and that this reduction was brought about by medical improvements – new medical techniques, more and better doctors and more hospitals.

In the 1950s this view was challenged from two angles. First, Connell (1951), having previously attributed the increase of Irish population in the eighteenth century primarily to an increase in the birth rate, drew attention to the anomaly of attributing opposing explanations for the same phenomenon on either side of the Irish Channel, and suggested that the possibility of explaining the rise in the rate of growth of English population in terms of a rising birth rate might be explored. This suggestion was taken up by Habakkuk. He considered the possible consequences of the increase of resources and the demand for labour, and concluded that

> the acceleration of population growth was primarily the result of specifically economic changes, and in particular of an increase in the demand for labour. This still leaves open the mode of operation of this increased demand. Was its principal effect to lower the age at marriage, and in this way to increase births? Or to increase the ability of the labourers to feed their children? (Habakkuk, 1953, 133)

Habakkuk's opinion was that the first effect was the more important, and that 'the increased demand operated more via the birth-rate than the death-rate'. These suggestions have found support from subsequent writers. Starting from the assertion that 'pre-industrial Western fertility was generally limited to economic considerations', Krause (1959, 528, 537) went on to state that 'there is reason to believe that favourable economic conditions brought about an increase of nuptiality and a decrease of family limitation'. Deane and Cole, relying on the parish register returns, take the view that

> the decline in mortality played a smaller part in the expansion of population during the Industrial Revolution than has sometimes been supposed, and that the dramatic fall in the death rate came after the population upsurge had passed its peak. (Deane and Cole, 1962, 133)

To account for the rise of population before the death rate fell, they assert that

> the expansion of population in those districts which felt the direct influence of industrial growth was much more clearly due to an increased birth rate. .... It seems clear that the rise in the birth rate was closely connected with the process of industrialisation, although it remains an open question whether this increase took place primarily as a result of earlier marriage, greater fertility, or even an increase in illegitimacy. (Deane and Cole, 1962, 133-4)

The common thread running through most of the arguments in favour of a rising birth rate in the eighteenth century is the essentially Malthusian proposition that, for the mass of the labouring population, there is a positive correlation between incomes and births. 'The reward of labour,' Adam Smith observed, 'must necessarily encourage in such a manner the marriage and multiplication of labourers, as may enable them to supply that continually increasing demand by a continually increasing population.' 'What is essentially necessary,' wrote Malthus, 'to a rapid increase of population is a great and continued demand for labour.' 'Is it not evident,' asked Arthur Young, 'that demand for hands, that is employment, must regulate the numbers of the people?' (All quoted by Habakkuk, 1953, 118.) The view that birth rate tends to rise in response to a rise of incomes (or increased opportunities for children's employment, or a system of poor relief incorporating family allowances) is one from which there have always been some dissenters, and the speculations of Smith, Malthus and Young may be matched by others from contemporary writers taking contrary views. (Eversley, 1959)

There is, without doubt, a correlation, in the short run, between incomes and marriages and births. Weather changes from season to season affect harvests, and harvest fluctuations affect food prices and farmers' incomes. The vagaries of the weather alternately distribute hardship and plenty to different economic groups in society according as they suffer or benefit from high or low prices; and there is ample evidence of a quick reaction by marriage and birth rates to temporary improvements or deteriorations in economic circumstances. But there is very little evidence that, apart from the perennial round of harvest fluctuations, there was any long-run trend in the weather in the eighteenth century which could have had any influence on long-run trends in the birth rate. (Manley, 1952, 296–307)

The evidence relating to trends in incomes in the eighteenth century is reviewed in Chapter IV. Though there were periods when incomes rose for different classes in different parts of the country, there is no general trend in incomes which could be said to correspond to the trend in population growth: indeed, the period of most rapid population growth towards the end of the eighteenth century and in the early nineteenth century was one of stagnant or even falling real wages. The hypothesis that higher incomes increase birth rates is difficult to confirm from eighteenth-century evidence, and depends, in any case, upon rising real incomes. It is not easy to show that these were rising sufficiently at the right periods to have accounted for the increase in the rate of growth of population, nor is it by any means certain that rising incomes would necessarily have led to higher birth rates.

The second angle of attack on Griffith's hypothesis of death rates falling as a result of medical improvements came from medical quarters. McKeown and Brown (1955) placed Griffith's 'medical improvements' under the microscope and found them wanting. They took the view that 'surgery had an almost inappreciable effect on vital statistics until the advent of anaesthesia and antiseptics'; that the introduction of 'institutional confinement had an adverse effect on mortality'; that the very few new drugs made available during the eighteenth century were unlikely to have had any very significant effect on mortality; that, because 'the chief indictment of hospital work at this period is not that it did no good, but that it positively did harm', the increase in the provision of hospitals is more likely to have increased rather than reduced mortality – 'it was not until much later that hospital patients could be reasonably certain of dying from the disease with which they were admitted'; and that 'it is hard to believe that inoculation can have been responsible for a reduction in the incidence of smallpox large enough to have had a substantial effect on national mortality trends'. These were fairly rigorous conclusions which cut away a lot of ground from under the falling death rate hypothesis. McKeown and Brown then examined the relative influences of birth and death rates on population growth: they observed that

> at the outset we should recognize that the probable influence of the two rates is mainly determined by their levels. When both rates are high it is very much easier to increase the population by reducing the death rate than by increasing the birth rate; when the rates are low the reverse is true. (1955, 127)

This exercise of elementary logic, combined with their conclusion that 'a substantial increase [in the birth rate] is unlikely to have occurred during the eighteenth century, except as a secondary result of a reduction in mortality', led them to believe, in spite of their strictures on 'medical improvements', that the probable explanation of the acceleration in the rate of growth of population lay in a falling death rate. They attributed this to 'improvement in the environment', that is to higher standards of housing, clothing, diet and nourishment.

Though there has been some reaction against the severity of McKeown and Brown's dismissal of 'medical improvements', in general both aspects of this argument have found fairly widespread acceptance. A study of life expectancies in the British peerage (Hollingsworth, 1965, 56–7) has revealed not only that there was a substantial increase in life expectancies in the eighteenth century but also that this increase was already apparent in the generation born after 1725. Habakkuk (1958 (1), 500) conceded that 'initially the increase in the second half of the eighteenth century must have been due simply to the absence of the exceptional causes of high mortality in the early part of the century'.

The present state of research still leaves, therefore, two rival hypotheses disputing the field. The rising birth rate hypothesis leans heavily on the parish register returns, accepts some decline in the death rate but places this in a later period, and tends to presuppose important economic changes mainly connected with industrialization: the falling death rate hypothesis, on the other hand, tends to pay little regard to the evidence of the parish registers, accepts some consequential rise in the birth rate, and draws on environmental, dietetical, epidemiological, prophylactic and, possibly, economic factors to explain the new trend. The latter school of thought therefore accords only a very slight role to prior economic changes as determinants of the rate of population growth, and gives greater prominence to non-economic factors.

> It seems clear that even where population growth was in some sense a response to autonomous economic changes, the most significant change was not any independent increase in *per capita* incomes, and that over most of Europe population growth was not in fact a response to economic changes even in a more general sense. There is a case, therefore, for regarding the population growth as in some measure fortuitous. (Habakkuk, 1963, 612–13)

Both schools of thought need to take account of the possible chronological complication implicit in the work of Tucker and Youngson. The birth rate hypothesis is less likely to accept the possibility of an early upturn in the rate of growth of population, since most of the economic trends on which it relies were features of later rather than earlier in the century.

Of the possible explanations, in short, only one – that of the death rate beginning to fall not later than the middle decades of the century – really satisfies the conditions for a 'cause' of subsequent economic growth, if only on the key ground of chronological priority. And even this explanation may invoke *some* pre-existing economic growth. In the remainder of this chapter, population growth as a possible stimulus to economic growth must therefore be pursued on the basis of just one of a range of possible explanations of the acceleration in the rate of growth of population. The other explanations may be inherently as acceptable, or more acceptable; but because of their particular chronologies or the nature of their relationship to economic and social development, they are far less relevant to a discussion of the origins of the Industrial Revolution.

Assuming, on these grounds, and solely for the sake of the analysis of origins, that population growth began to accelerate in the first half of the eighteenth century partly as a consequence of non-economic changes and partly of gradual economic growth, we can now proceed to consider the possible consequences for economic growth of a prior rise in the rate of growth of population.

The tendency in population theory has most commonly been to regard population as a dependent variable – one which comes into operation as a consequence of some prior economic change. Once set in motion it tends to become a brake on further progress, threatening to nullify the economic growth already initiated. With birth rates in the region of 40 per 1,000, and death rates, with the aid of modern preventive and curative medicine, under 20 or even 15 per 1,000, population growth can amount to as much as $2\frac{1}{2}$ per cent per year, requiring a comparable rate of economic growth if *per capita* real income is not to fall; and a $2\frac{1}{2}$ per cent rate of economic growth is not easily sustained in a backward economy. Whatever problems for growth may be created in this way for underdeveloped countries in the mid-twentieth century, however, population has seldom achieved and never sustained these growth rates in the past.

> In no country except the United States and Canada – where vast empty lands cried out to be filled – did rise in income stimulate population growth remotely approaching that which Malthusian theory indicates rising income should induce. In no case except those of 'empty lands' did the rate of population growth exceed 17·5 per cent per decade even for a single decade. The median peak decade rate among [13 selected] countries is 12·5 per cent. The median rate for the 50 years of fastest growth is much lower. (Hagen, 1959, 315)

Since total real output is estimated to have multiplied $2\frac{1}{2}$-fold during the eighteenth century, while population increased by only 66 per cent, there is no question of population growth having eroded economic growth in eighteenth-century Britain, whatever the situation may have been in the early nineteenth century; and it may be worth noting, as a first conclusion, that, in spite of a clear acceleration in the rate of growth, the still relatively slow overall growth of population kept the Malthusian barrier conveniently at arm's length in the long run over the early stages of industrialization.

In the present context, however, the extent to which population growth is a dependent variable is an irrelevance. We can only be concerned with population growth as an exogenous stimulant to economic growth. There are many possible ways in which population increase may have favourable repercussions on the rate of economic development. For example,

> an abundant supply of labour at the going wage was favourable to accumulation, on the assumption that profits were much the main source of accumulation; and in a period when there were considerable obstacles to interregional labour movements, a high rate of natural increase was a necessary condition of an abundant supply of labour. Population increase was therefore favourable to the widening of capital and so increased the opportunities of trying out new methods which might be independently available; i.e. it led to a more rapid absorption of existing technical knowledge and therefore increased the chances of making further technical progress. (Habakkuk, 1963, 614)

The evidence in the second half of the eighteenth century certainly seems to point to a surplus of labour rather than to a shortage. While the recruitment of labour in some of the out-of-the-way sites selected for some of the early textile factories may have raised some problems, these were problems of the mobility of labour rather than of its overall scarcity. Of course, it is not wholly true that industrialization was accomplished in eighteenth-century Britain without some increase of real wages. The wage trends discussed in Chapter IV indicate some response by wages to the growing demand for industrial labour. Rising wages, particularly in the north of England in the first half of the century, are commonly explained in terms of the increased demand for industrial labour. But after the middle of the century the more rapid growth of population would appear, in the main, to have met all the demands for labour, and industrial employment expanded without any marked rise in the price of labour. The multiplication of productive units, using current techniques and able to draw heavily upon labour resources without driving up the price of labour, was a principal feature of industrialization in eighteenth-century Britain. On the other hand, it is also possible that an ample supply of labour at the going wage might have tended to discourage the adoption of new techniques more important in the long run for economic growth.

While an abundant population may, in the early stages, have favoured accumulation, it tended to be unfavourable to a high degree of mechanisation. It made it easier for the capitalist to accumulate, but it encouraged him to adopt the techniques which required a considerable amount of labour in relation to capital. . . . In brief, abundant labour induces [entrepreneurs] to adopt those techniques which, on balance, are least likely to develop rapidly in the future, techniques which do not build up a body of skill and experience. (Habakkuk, 1958 (2), 32–3, 35)

The experience of the abundant and cheap supply of, say, handloom weavers in all branches of textile manufacture may well have been a factor in the relative slowness of the adoption of power-loom weaving; but, in general, the swift pace of technological advance during the British Industrial Revolution shows surprisingly little evidence of being impeded by a super-abundance of cheap labour.

Secondly, 'a growing population might stimulate investment by its effects on the demand side. Even if *per capita* incomes fell, there would be an increase in total demand if the rise in the population was less than the fall in *per capita* incomes' (Habakkuk, 1963, 614).

The problem of the connection between rising population and aggregate demand is investigated more fully in Chapter IV. There is little likelihood that real incomes of any major group fell other than briefly for most of the eighteenth century, at least up to the outbreak of war in 1793, and the demand pull from growing population, far from being damped down by declining *per capita* income, was reinforced for long periods by rising real incomes.

Thirdly, 'a growing population is likely to spend a higher proportion of its income on housing and transport facilities' (Habakkuk, 1963, 614).

This tendency is encouraged by urban concentration, which makes it worth while to create and improve these services. The absence of census information for the eighteenth century makes it impossible to produce statistical confirmation of trends in urbanization, but it is almost certainly true that towns were growing disproportionately fast – that an ever-increasing proportion of the population was living in towns. Against a national population increase of 66 per cent during the century, Manchester's population is estimated to have risen from about 9,000 to 70,000, Birmingham's from possibly 15,000 to nearly 70,000 and Glasgow's from 12,000 to 84,000. These and many other comparable urban developments created many entirely new categories of investment during the eighteenth century. This was the period, for example, of the beginnings of the numerous 'improvement commissions', by means of which an effective start was made with the paving, lighting, policing and sewerage of towns. No estimates are available of the total investment in these 'improvements', but there can be little doubt that it increased substantially in successive decades from the middle of the century. The urban concentration of population and industry began, too, almost for the first time, to make the improvement of transport services solely to meet the needs of towns economically attractive. The first Bridgewater canal of 1759, for example, was built primarily to enable a coalowner (the Duke himself) to take advantage of a growing urban demand for coal, while its larger extension of 1763 to connect Manchester to Liverpool was planned more with a view to the mixed traffic arising from a large inland town than to the specialized needs of a cotton industry drawing its raw material wholly through a west coast port, since this trade was still on a relatively small scale when the canal was planned. The provincial newspaper, another new feature of the eighteenth century, was an urban development, and the facility of advertising in this medium, increasingly taken up by businessmen in this century, indicates that to some extent they were beginning to think in terms of potential mass urban markets. It must remain a moot point, however, how far the investment and expenditure stimulated in these ways represented additional investment and expenditure or merely transfers from other sectors. To the extent that the latter was the case, the net stimulus to growth may have been minimal.

Fourthly, 'a stable population restricts the opportunity for youth in industry, [and] produces old and unadventurous leadership' (Kindleberger, 1964, 71).

Conversely, an expanding population created opportunities for youthful energy and uninhibited innovation. It is unlikely that sufficient information will ever be made available to enable us to judge whether or not the growing population was offering wider opportunities for youthful entrepreneurship in eighteenth-century Britain. In so far as the increase in the rate of growth of population was the product of a falling death rate, and since this reduced mortality was concentrated in the lowest age groups, the average age of the population in general may have been lowered during the century. Whether this involved a general reduction in the ages at which entrepreneurs and other innovators emerged, with a corresponding increase in the level of energy and adventurousness, is extremely difficult to judge. Without a wider base for comparison between the entrepreneurs of the Industrial Revolution and those of earlier periods, it is clearly not possible to generalize about this point.

Fifthly,

> since transformation occurs more readily at the margin than within it, an increasing population is more readily redirected into new industries, more effectively trained for new tasks. Two children per family, a boy and a girl, replace the father and mother and maintain the existing economic structure. With more children, there is the necessity to redirect resources and pressure to create more economic opportunities. (Kindleberger, 1964, 71)

Here, too, the necessary statistical data to test the validity of this proposition in eighteenth-century society is totally lacking. Certain trends are, however, suggestive. The very fact that population grew at an increasing rate, and that this involved a disproportionately fast rate of urbanization implies some increase in the general geographical mobility of population. Similarly, even the relatively gradual economic growth of the earlier decades of the eighteenth century involved increasing industrialization; the proportion of the population engaged in industry was almost certainly higher in, say, 1760 than it had been in 1700. This, in its turn, implies increasing occupational mobility. Though it is seldom possible to test the hypothesis against known biographies, it seems inherently likely that an increased number of children graduating from families in the traditional occupations (farming, woollen manufacture, small-scale domestic metal-ware manufacture) would tend to increase the flow of labour available for – even clamouring for – employment in the more rapidly expanding new industries. At least one of the great institutions of eighteenth-century society – the poor law – was geared, through the system of pauper apprenticeship, to filling this role. Though increased geographical and occupational mobility may have done little actually to stimulate economic growth, it tended to facilitate growth, or may, at a slightly more positive level, have removed previously existing impediments to growth.

Finally, 'a growing population might also stimulate investment by reducing the risks of entrepreneurial error' (Habakkuk, 1963, 614). Similarly, the steady widening of the market resulting from persistent population growth encourages entrepreneurs to think in terms of expanding rather than constant markets. This is particularly true in the growing towns, where the existence of more highly organized and easily accessible markets (in both the institutional and economic senses of the word) increasingly simplifies the problems of distribution and encourages entrepreneurs to aim for the economies of large-scale production and distribution. A growing population or one growing more rapidly than formerly offers proportionately greater incentive to create additional capacity by innovation or the employment of more productive techniques.

Few of these mechanisms would, on their own, probably have contributed very significantly to economic expansion. Together, however, they may have added up to a useful impetus to growth. The stimulus would, from its nature, be fairly gradual, though it must make its greatest impact at the period of most marked acceleration of population growth. On the hypothesis adopted above – that the increased rate of population growth was initiated mainly by reduced mortality rates in the middle decades of the century – population growth may thus have contributed to the stimulus to economic expansion at a critical phase.

On the other hand, there may be ways in which an increase of population might tend to inhibit economic growth. For example, if the population growth occurred chiefly as a result of a reduction in death rates, such a reduction was likely (in the circumstances of the eighteenth century) to have its principal effect on infant mortality, thus increasing the proportion of dependent population, which in turn would tend to increase the proportion of income which is consumed, reducing savings proportionately.

The balance between those forces making for growth and those tending towards stagnation depends upon the economic environment of the population growth. Habakkuk (1958 (2), 30–1) has noted three sets of circumstances which must be present if population growth is to induce economic growth. There must already be a high rate of savings; there must be an abundant supply of productive land either at home or overseas; and there must already have been some previous economic growth which had created a class of experienced entrepreneurs. Other chapters in this book discuss the extent to which these conditions existed in late eighteenth-century Britain. Given their existence to some degree, and the presence of other favourable factors such as the easy availability of raw materials, potential overseas markets and a capital supply capable of expansion – factors present in eighteenth-century Britain, but not, for example, in Ireland in the same period – there is a good chance that population growth would be more of a stimulus to growth than the reverse.

In general, however, population growth is so closely interwoven with economic expansion that it must remain exceedingly difficult to distinguish cause from effect in the pattern of development. Of the whole range of hypotheses for a model of demographic economic development, the majority tie population growth closely and dependently to economic growth: even the models of autonomous population growth turn out on closer inspection to be partly dependent on some form of prior economic growth. 'This is simply to say that growth is a positive feedback process in which more growth helps population expansion, which in turn supports growth – if nothing interrupts' (Kindleberger, 1964, 82).

In eighteenth-century Britain nothing did interrupt. Though the positive contribution of population growth *per se* to the Industrial Revolution may not easily or convincingly be demonstrable, an analysis of this particular instance of rapid growth which left out the demographic contribution would clearly be incomplete.

III
The Financial Origins

Theoretical studies of economic growth commonly place capital accumulation and investment at the core of their analyses. It follows that these aspects of growth should also be central features of any study of the Industrial Revolution, for it is clear that, whatever the actual rates involved, net investment stepped up to a new plateau towards the end of the eighteenth century. The methods of production employed in many industries in the pre-Industrial Revolution era involved extraordinarily little capital equipment. Domestic industry was, by definition, carried on in the home, and few of the items of machinery or equipment – spinning wheels, looms, knitting frames or nailing anvils – cost more than a few shillings or, at most, a few pounds. With these early techniques, economic expansion was achieved through the multiplication of low-capital units and could be accomplished at a very low level of net investment. There were, of course, heavier industries such as shipbuilding, mining and the metallurgical industries, with proportionately greater capital requirements. But so long as ships were timber-built, mines relatively shallow and furnaces relatively small, production in these industries tended to remain labour- rather than capital-intensive. A principal feature of the Industrial Revolution was the substitution of capital for labour as powered machinery replaced the old hand-driven units in the textile industries and took over some of the heavier tasks from men and animals in the mining and metal industries.

If the problem of investment in the Industrial Revolution was largely ignored by the earlier historians, it was principally because of their preoccupation with description at the expense of analysis, and more recent studies have done much to redress the balance. Rostow, for example, has indicated that a stepping-up of the level of net investment to 10 per cent of the national product is essential if growth is to be self-sustaining. The processes by which a society's rate of saving is increased, and the capital thus accumulated translated into the fixed assets of industrial production are complex, and must be examined with some care.

In the field of industry alone, however, it is easy to exaggerate the scale of the need for capital. Expanding industry requires two kinds of capital, fixed (investment in buildings and machinery) and variable (investment in stocks of raw materials, goods in the process of manufacture, unsold finished goods and trade credit to customers). Capital invested in fixed assets must be met by very long-term, or irredeemable loans, which may, however, be transferable: capital invested in the variable assets may be supplied from relatively short-term loans, since goods in the pipeline will ultimately be sold, and debts repaid. The latter requirement can therefore be met largely by short-term credit, for which purpose the bill of exchange, coupled with discounting facilities, is admirably designed; and Ashton has shown how widespread was the use of such bills in the eighteenth-century economy (1955, 185–7). Because of the virtually irredeemable nature of capital locked up in machinery, bricks and mortar, fixed investment raised problems of a different order. Apart from capital accumulated through the systematic allowance for depreciation – and eighteenth-century business accountancy took little or no account of this – fixed assets must be financed by the creation of new capital. In practice, fixed capital tended to represent a relatively small proportion of total capital requirements in British industry of the eighteenth century, the proportion varying commonly between 5 and 10 per cent of the total in the early and mid-eighteenth century, rising to above 50 per cent in some of the larger textile undertakings of the later eighteenth century. (Pollard, 1964, 301–3)

Variable capital, however, is still capital which must be met by savings – the foregoing of current consumption – in the same way as fixed capital: and so far as economic growth is concerned the level of aggregate investment is the significant variable. The effective difference between the two types of investment lies simply in the ease with which the respective needs can be met. The relatively high liquidity of loans for variable capital makes them a far more attractive type of loan to prospective lenders, while the risk (not to mention the unlimited liability for debts before the coming of limited liability in the mid-nineteenth century) of fixed investment created an entirely different category of loan.

Moreover, since the problem we are investigating is one of industrial growth, it is desirable to allocate neither too much nor too little influence to capital investment as a means of stimulating increased productivity. There is a tendency to assume that increased output or increased output per head are simply functions of the level of investment. But output and productivity are affected by more than merely the quantity of net investment – the input of labour, technology and entrepreneurial skill are also relevant.

The slow and continuous increase in time of the national supply of productive means and of savings is obviously an important factor in explaining the course of economic history through the centuries, but it is completely overshadowed by the fact that development consists primarily in employing existing resources in a different way, in doing new things with them, irrespective of whether those resources increase or not. (Schumpeter, 1934, 68)

There seems no reason to suppose that capital accumulation does by itself exercise so predominant an influence on economic development. . . . Whatever may have been true in the past, it is now technical innovation – the introduction of new and cheaper ways of doing things – that dominates economic progress. Whether technical innovation, in the sectors of the economy in which it occurs, makes large demands on capital is, however, very doubtful. Many innovations can be given effect to in the course of capital replacement out of depreciation allowances, which, in an expanding economy, may be fully as large as net savings. Others may actually reduce the stock of capital required. (Cairncross, 1955, 235, 237)

Depreciation itself is, of course, a form of saving for future investment, while the higher the rate of accumulation the greater the likelihood that new techniques will be taken up on a massive scale as soon as they become available. In a study of the increases in productivity in the United States between 1869 and 1953, Abramovitz discovered that had the productivity of all resources remained constant during this period, the increase in resources per head (mainly capital) would only have produced a rise of 14 per cent in net national product *per capita*. Since net national product *per capita* quadrupled during this period, by far the greater part of the increase in wealth was to be accounted for in terms of rises of productivity of these resources. Some part of this enormous difference was attributable to the inadequacy of some of the statistics, but

when all due allowance for the concealed increase in resource expansion has been made, however, there will remain a huge area to be explained as an increase in productivity. Our capital stock of knowledge concerning the organization and technique of production has grown at a phenomenal pace. A portion of this increase – presumably an increasing proportion – is due to an investment of resources in research, education, and the like. This part we may possibly be able to attribute accurately to the input of these resources insofar as we learn to trace the connection between such investment in knowledge and its marginal social contribution, as distinct from those small parts of its value which can be privately appropriated. Beyond this, however, lies the gradual growth of applied knowledge which is, no doubt, the result of human activity, but not of that kind of activity involving costly choice which we think of as economic input. To identify the causes which explain not only the rate at which our opportunities to raise efficiency increase but also the pace at which we take advantage of those opportunities will, no doubt, remain the central problem in both the history and theory of our economic growth. (Abramovitz, 1956, 13–14)

Nonetheless, extensive investment is needed to implement the new techniques of production constantly coming forward. Of the two problems thus distinguished – the accumulation of capital, and the raising of productivity through advances in technology – the former only will be considered in this chapter, while the latter forms the subject of Chapter V.

Capital investment of itself, then, can account for only a small share of the increases in productivity which lie at the core of rapid economic growth. But this is not to consign capital accumulation to an insignificant role in an industrial revolution. To do so would be to confuse *per capita* growth with aggregate growth. Both types of growth must take place, the latter particularly in a period of rapid population growth. If capital alone plays a relatively small part in raising productivity, substantial investment is simultaneously required to expand productive capacity (at existing levels of productivity) merely to keep pace with the increasing demand of a growing population. The scope for investment, in other words, is two-dimensional: investment in depth produces increases in the productivity of the factors of production, while investment in breadth copes with the multiplication of units of production using current techniques of production. There was also the likelihood that the demand for industrial capital would be inflated by sheer wastage:

In Britain, the real costs of industrialization were greatly increased by the inevitable misapplication of resources, false starts, errors and rapid obsolescence inevitable in a pioneer economy. The badly planned towns and transport networks were, perhaps, among the most costly tributes paid to experience. (Pollard, 1958, 219)

The scale of industry, however, even at the height of the Industrial Revolution, was still sufficiently small for its capital requirements not to raise insuperable barriers. If the British Industrial Revolution had consisted of no more than industrial growth, there would be little need for intensive investigation of the sources of capital: an economy must be far less advanced than was the British economy of the mid-eighteenth century to be unable to generate the relatively small amounts of capital required to finance industrial expansion at this stage. What raised capital formation to the forefront of the economic problems associated with the Industrial Revolution was the fact that the industrial demand for capital was but one of a range of demands being made simultaneously on the national supply of capital. And among these competing sources of demand for capital, industry may conceivably not have been the greatest.

The competing demands came from investment in turnpike roads, in inland navigation (at first river navigation, later canals), enclosures, housing and other social overheads. Each of these sectors of invest-ment was substantial, and followed its own chronology. In 1836, for example, turnpike toll income amounted to £1·6 million annually. At, say, 5 per cent, this would represent a total accumulated capital of £32 million. Of this, mortgage debts of the turnpike trusts accounted in 1836 for £9 million. In Scotland, the Commissioners for Highland Roads and Bridges alone built over 1,000 bridges and 920 miles of roads between 1803 and 1820 at a cost of between £400 and £450 per mile. Of the £½ million spent in this way, half came from the govern-ment, and the rest from local landowners. £376,650 is known to have been invested in river navigation between 1600 and 1750, but it is likely that the actual investment was greatly in excess of this figure, and it continued even after the coming of canals. So far as canal investment is concerned, eighty canal companies had a paid-up capital of £13·2 million in 1825. The parliamentary and legal costs of enclosure tended to vary between about 5s and £5 per acre, and to have increased steadily during the second half of the eighteenth century: over the whole period they may have averaged 20–25s per acre. To these costs should be added the expense of actually making the enclosure, which, on average, equalled the parliamentary and legal costs. At this rate the

3·2 million acres estimated to have been enclosed between 1761 and 1801 might have involved an investment in the region of £7 million. The chronologies of these different fields of investment are even harder to estimate than the totals invested. While investment in turnpike roads may conceivably have reached a peak in the middle decades of the eighteenth century, diminishing the demand for capital by the period of heavier industrial investment in the later decades of the century, investment in inland navigation and enclosures, already high in the third quarter of the century, rose rapidly in the last quarter.

Nor was private enterprise, in the shape of industry, turnpike trusts, canal companies or landlords, the sole borrower in the capital market. By the beginning of the eighteenth century the government had entered the field of long-term borrowing. The Crown had, of course, always borrowed extensively in the short-term market, and continued to do so throughout the eighteenth century. An important new feature of the eighteenth-century capital market was the growth of the permanent national debt. In spite of attempts to eliminate or reduce this debt by sinking funds, each successive war in the eighteenth century stepped the debts up to a new plateau. From £46 million in 1739, the War of Austrian Succession drove it up to £75 million, the Seven Years' War to £132 million and the War of American Independence to over £200 million. At the outbreak of the French War in 1793 the debt stood at £244 million, a figure which more than doubled before peace was signed in 1802. During the half century between the outbreak of the Seven Years' War and the Peace of Amiens, government borrowing reduced by about £10 million every year the capital available for economic expansion.

Unlike investment in the private sector, government borrowing in the eighteenth century was largely unproductive. Though some of the borrowing went into fixed assets in naval dockyards, the overwhelmingly greater part of it simply met current expenditure in wartime, much of it overseas. So far as economic growth was concerned, this was capital lost.

Nor did these successive increases to the permanent national debt represent the whole of the effective drainage of capital from more productive investment in this period. For another feature of the market in government loans in the eighteenth century was international borrowing. Throughout the first two-thirds of the eighteenth century a growing proportion of the permanent national debt was held by Dutch investors. This Dutch-held portion, which might have amounted to between £25 million and £30 million in 1783, was heavily reduced in the course of the next two decades. Since the national debt was not merely not reduced during this period, but substantially increased, it follows that British capital was found to replace the Dutch loans to an extent that represented a further drain on the home capital market. This additional demand also coincided with the period of accelerating industrial growth.

In comparison with these various figures, it has been estimated (Habakkuk and Deane, 1963, 75) that investment in the cotton industry between 1783 and 1802 amounted to about £8 million, while the 215 blast furnaces said to be in existence in 1806 (and representing probably at least half the total investment in the iron industry) represented a capital of about £11 million. Investment in the expanding coal industry in this period must have been relatively heavy, while the growth in other industries – building, shipbuilding, engineering, textiles other than cotton, for example – must also have been significant. And when it is borne in mind that variable capital in most of these industries probably equalled or exceeded the fixed capital (which is all that Habakkuk and Deane's estimate takes into account) it may be that their conclusion (p. 76) that 'there is thus no evidence that the industries which are said to have "ignited" the Industrial Revolution had had much effect on the national rate of capital formation by the beginning of the nineteenth century' underestimates the significance of industrial investment in the early stages of the Industrial Revolution.

But industrial investment cannot be meaningfully abstracted from the whole field of investment. With the exception of government borrowing, all investment in the second half of the eighteenth century contributed to different aspects of economic growth. Though statistics for its measurement are not available, it is clear that in the aggregate this demand for capital expanded significantly in the late eighteenth century to a degree that placed capital accumulation on an entirely new plane. The economic history of the late eighteenth century bears witness to the extent to which this challenge was met. In these circumstances, the generation of additional capital, and its channelling into productive investment must represent important elements in any analysis of the origins of the Industrial Revolution.

The problem of industrial investment in eighteenth-century Britain, then, was twofold: how was the supply of capital for all purposes increased? and by what means was this increased supply channelled into productive investment?

There is no prima facie necessity to demonstrate an increase in savings. It was not beyond the bounds of possibility for the whole of the additional investment in the eighteenth century to have been met from hoards or the diversion of existing savings into new forms of investment. Nevertheless, in view of the immensity of the investment of the later decades of the eighteenth century, this possibility is unlikely to be the correct explanation. Some increase in saving is almost certain to have occurred. Unless there were significant changes in the propensity to save of the wealthier classes in eighteenth-century society (some evidence for which is discussed below), any marked increase in aggregate capital formation must have come from the savings of those whose incomes were growing faster than the average. Only a minority of the population, in any case, enjoyed incomes sufficiently great to permit saving. Most of the incomes in this category would derive from land, commerce, industry and gilt-edged stocks (government bonds, East India, South Sea and various forms of annuities).

Savings out of income from stock-holding are not 'new' savings, since they depend on some prior savings. On the other hand, a significant proportion of industrial investment at all times is drawn from ploughed-back profits, and there is no doubt that at least some of the capital that financed the Industrial Revolution came directly from the accumulated profits of earlier industry. This is simply to insist that a proportion of industrial expansion is always based on prior industrial growth – that rapid industrial expansion cannot begin in a stagnating economy. In fact, of course, the drift of all research since Mantoux into the economic history of the eighteenth century has been to demonstrate the existence of this 'prior' growth.

But, while 'normal' industrial growth might be financed predominantly from this source, it is less easy to explain a sudden spurt of industrial investment in these terms; nor can the vast and necessary increase in non-industrial investment be explained other than marginally in this way. The decisive change in the nature of industrial growth in the late eighteenth century was the sharp spurts of growth in some new industries or new technologies in older industries. The cotton industry, for example, where it was not wholly a new growth, was built on the foundations of the fustian or linen industries. Both the latter were domestically organized and unlikely to generate capital through accumulation of profits in the hands of those who would reinvest in factories to house the new powered machines. Thus the key sectors of industrial expansion in the Industrial Revolution – engineering, canal-making, iron-making by the new techniques of coke-smelting, puddling and rolling, in addition to cotton manufacture – were the very ones least likely to have access to the traditional source of capital in ploughed-back profits. We are left, therefore, with trade and land as the most likely sources of additional savings in the middle and later eighteenth century.

Overseas trade was almost certainly growing faster than the national product during most of the eighteenth century: and within the whole field of trade, certain sectors, particularly those concerned with the transatlantic and re-export trades, grew abnormally fast in some periods. Without doubt, the more-than-average growth of mercantile profits was an important source of capital for late eighteenth-century economic expansion. It is possible to trace innumerable examples of the translation of mercantile profits into industrial investment – the capital for the Coalbrookdale enterprise put up by Darby's Bristol merchant partners; David Dale's accumulated profits as an importer of linen yarn turned into the famous New Lanark cotton mill; or the capital of the Liverpool merchants which created the Weaver and Sankey Brook navigations on which the Merseyside salt industry was based. This source of industrial capital has been stressed most explicitly in relation to the slave trade and its accompanying West African and West Indian trades. 'The profits obtained [from these trades] provided one of the main streams of that accumulation of capital in England which financed the Industrial Revolution' (Williams, 1944, 52). This is an extremely difficult hypothesis to substantiate. Williams's argument is made by the juxtaposition of the two sets of facts – those relating to the slave trade, and those relating to the Industrial Revolution – rather than by detailed analysis of the process of interaction. There are some examples, of course, of slave traders and sugar-importers (the principal trade based on slave plantations in the eighteenth century) turning their profits into industrial capital. But the only real example of this type of transfer quoted by Williams is the case of Anthony Bacon, the London merchant who set up major ironworks in South Wales: his other examples are all drawn from the fields of banking and insurance, where the link with industry is more tenuous. And even in Bacon's case it is doubtful whether the profits of his slave trading or slave-based trades can be separated from the profits of other, legitimate trade he may also have carried on. On the other hand, there are instances – those of William Beckford, or the Pinneys, for example – where the trading profits were largely sunk in landed acres and stately homes.

Two elements are involved in estimating the role of slave-based profits in the finance of the British economic expansion of the eighteenth century: one is the proportion of total British trade made up by the slave trade and the trade in slave-produced commodities; and the other is the proportion of industrial capital which was drawn from trading profits. If, for the sake of argument, it is assumed that both these proportions were one-fifth, then the share of industrial investment generated by slavery and the slave trade would be a mere 4 per cent. Obviously *some* industrial capital came from this source, but it must remain questionable whether it ever rose to very significant levels.

The problem of the profits of the slave trade is simply one aspect of the general question of the correlation between the growth of mercantile profits and an increase in industrial investment. The first goal of many a merchant was the acquisition of a landed estate with a stately home, and an unknown proportion of all mercantile profits in the eighteenth century was poured into this form of conspicuous consumption. True, capital spent on buying land passed into the hands of the seller, who might invest it productively, but capital spent on the construction of stately homes made a less direct contribution to economic development. However, the ability of the mercantile class to sterilize its savings in this way was restricted in the late eighteenth century by a shortage of suitable estates coming on the market.

> By the second half of the eighteenth century English landownership had settled down into a fairly stable pattern. The main element of change was the constant infusion of new landed proprietors from trade, industry, and the professions, but the limited amount of land available for purchase meant that such newcomers were less numerous than at any time in the two previous centuries. (Mingay, 1963, 47)

It is even possible that in the second half of the century the drying-up of the land market, perhaps in part a consequence of the much wider use than formerly of entail and strict settlement, was forcing into the capital market savings hitherto funnelled into unproductive uses.

While it remains true, therefore, that expanding mercantile profits must have contributed to the increased accumulation of capital in the second half of the eighteenth century, it is apparent that only a small proportion of these savings found its way into industry. The exact proportion cannot, for obvious reasons, be calculated. In default of this knowledge we must be careful not to exaggerate the importance of this source of capital. On the other hand, there is sufficient evidence of the participation of landowners in industry, either actively or passively, to make it quite clear that capital accumulated from rents played a significant role in the finance of eighteenth-century development. Since wealth surplus to normal consumption requirements was so highly concentrated in the landed class, if more capital was to be made available for economic expansion, it was from this class above all that it must come. Moreover, of all the sectoral incomes in the second half of the eighteenth century, it was the incomes of this class that appear to have risen most rapidly. Mingay estimates (1963, 51) that estate revenues rose about 40 or 50 per cent between 1760 and 1790, and where land was enclosed the gains appear to have been even greater. An estimate for Scotland (seemingly rather exaggerated) suggests an eightfold rise in rents between 1750 and 1815 (Campbell, 1965, 153), and it is clear that in Scotland a high proportion of the investment in agriculture and transport improvements came from the landowners. Where landlords sought industrial employment for their capital, the industries they turned to were generally those most intimately connected with the land – the extractive and metallurgical industries. The Earl of Balcarres, for example, entered a partnership with a Wigan ironmaster, James Corbett, in 1788 to develop the coal and iron resources of his Lancashire estates. Similarly, Lord Penrhyn invested the accumulated rents of his estates to develop the North Wales slate quarrying industry from the 1760s, while in 1777 the Earl of Elgin laid out what was claimed to be the largest private limeworks in Britain on the shores of the Firth of Forth at Rosyth.

There were, of course, important fields of industry in the late eighteenth century – particularly textiles – which drew little or no capital from landed sources, but in general terms there is much truth in the assertion that the increase in rents, itself mainly the product of enclosures and population pressure which drove up agricultural prices, may well have been a major factor in financing the Industrial Revolution.

Since so much of the surplus income above normal consumption requirements was concentrated in the landed class, changes in the habits of consumption of this class could have a significant effect upon their savings. It was a characteristic of this class to spend a high proportion of its income above what was required for current consumption on building stately homes. Virtually every landed family built a stately home; some built several; others rebuilt from time to time. Not a few indulged this form of conspicuous consumption to the extent of bankrupting themselves in the process. In the mid-twentieth century, in contrast, it is no longer the fashion for the wealthy classes to spend in this particular way: there are very few twentieth-century stately homes. Sometime between the early eighteenth century and the twentieth century there has been a diversion of the spending habits of the wealthy classes away from this form of unproductive investment. Some, at least, of the capital thus saved may have been turned to more productive uses. The chronology of trends in investment in stately homes may therefore have some relevance for the freeing of capital for more productive uses.

No attempt has so far been made to establish a chronology of stately home investment, and the task may turn out to be virtually impossible, bearing in mind the difficulty of dating the many hundreds, if not thousands, of houses involved, as well as of establishing at this distance of time the total expenditure on each building. But the difficulty in measuring this investment does not alter the fact that the trend may be important. Pevsner's *Buildings of England* series (Penguin Books), which describes and dates (either exactly or approximately) most of the principal stately homes in England, county by county, makes a possible starting-point for a rough approximation. A check through half a dozen random volumes of this survey (Durham, Hertfordshire, Middlesex, Northumberland, Nottinghamshire and Suffolk) reveals two broad generalizations that are of interest. First, there were significant regional variations in the chronologies of stately home building; and, second, between 1660 and 1900 there were two major periods of this kind of building – from the 1690s to the 1730s, and from the 1790s to the 1830s. Though there was some revival during the 1750s, '60s and '70s, at no time between the 1730s and '90s did the level reach the peaks of the early decades of both eighteenth and nineteenth centuries. There was relatively little building after the 1830s. This evidence is, of course, far too shaky to serve as a basis for working generalizations, but it may be sufficient to indicate that there were significant fluctuations in this important variable, and that there may possibly have been some reduction in this source of capital consumption in the key half-century from 1740 to 1790 which freed capital for other employment.

A principal influence on the demand for capital is the rate of interest, and a striking feature of the eighteenth-century money market was the gradual but substantial reduction in the rate of interest on most types of loans.

In the early eighteenth century the abundance of loanable funds made it possible for finance ministers to reduce the interest paid to the creditors of the State. During the wars, the Government of William III had been obliged to offer 7 or 8 per cent (the Usury Laws did not apply to the State); but in 1717 the rate on the perpetual annuities was reduced to 5, and in 1727 to 4 per cent. Finally, in the 1750s, Pelham lowered it once more, and, by converting a number of issues into a single one, brought into being, in 1757, the 3 per cent Consolidated Stock which, for short, we call Consols. These conversions were not imposed on an unwilling public: they reflected, rather than initiated, a fall in the rate of interest in the community generally. (Ashton, 1948, 9)

These rates were all for government loans, and there can be little doubt that, in the late seventeenth century at least, they were enhanced to some extent by the element of risk attached to government securities. The Stop of the Exchequer of 1672 was not quickly forgotten. Until at least the end of the War of Spanish Succession in 1713, the sheer inadequacy of government revenue in the face of wartime financial needs perpetuated the high degree of uncertainty attached to government loans. The restoration of financial stability and the establishment of a sounder constitutional basis for government finance in the period of peace following the Treaty of Utrecht in 1713 may, by eliminating the element of risk in lending to the government, have accounted for at least some of the fall in the rate of interest on government loans during the first three or four decades of the eighteenth century. There is some evidence, for example, that rates of interest on private land mortgages began to fall already before the end of the seventeenth century (Tucker, 1960, 31–2). There was, in addition, a tendency for rates of interest, under the pressure of heavier government borrowing, to rise during wartime. Thus, the increased frequency of wars in the second half of the eighteenth century tended to push the rate of interest abnormally high more frequently than in the earlier part of the century. All other things being equal, the most favourable period for borrowing in the eighteenth century was between the 1730s and the '50s. Though rates were penally high for only a few of the war years in the last quarter of the century, there were relatively few years when they were as low as they had been in times of peace before 1775, and it is clear that the period of most rapid economic growth was not, in fact, one in which capital was generally available at rates particularly favourable by eighteenth-century standards.

Nonetheless, the reduced rates of interest in the first half of the eighteenth century have clearly much relevance for economic growth.

> Lower rates brought into view many worthwhile projects, such as the improvement of town life, which could not otherwise have been undertaken because of their low rate of return as investments. (Pressnell, 1960, 181)

Given a general level of interest rates low enough to make investment in low-yield public works feasible, there was a close correlation between short-run fluctuations in interest rates and the level of activity in these fields.

> Public utility investment provides the clearest cases. This was marginal investment. . . . The overall picture is of sympathy between falling interest rates and high investment, at least at the major turning-points; there were bursts of activity around 1720 and 1726; in the early 'fifties; in the second half of the 'sixties and in the early 'seventies; and in the early 'nineties. (Pressnell, 1960, 190)

The same was true of investment in enclosures.

> There was a long period of relative inactivity from 1781 to 1795. . . . For more than a decade rates of interest were such as to make enclosure highly expensive, and for many impossible. (Ashton, 1955, 40–1)

For the businessman, on the other hand, as the prospective borrower of capital for commercial or industrial enterprises, the effect of variations in the rate of interest, whether in the short or the long run, is more difficult to assess. In general he was interested not so much in the actual level of the rate at any one point in time so much as in the difference between this rate and the marginal productivity of capital at that moment; and it was quite possible for business prospects to be so good that a relatively high marginal productivity of capital made borrowing attractive even at relatively high rates of interest, and vice versa. There may well be big disparities between rates of profit anticipated by businessmen considering potential projects in a period of economic expansion and the marginal changes in the level of interest rates. In an age when most industry tended to be relatively labour-intensive, even quite decisive changes in interest rates may have meant relatively little to the industrialist in terms of costs of production. In short, 'the significance of interest rates for industry and trade is one of the great unknowns of eighteenth-century history' (Pressnell, 1960, 195).

The relevance of changes in interest rates for eighteenth-century economic development appears, therefore, to be twofold – first, that the long-run decline early in the century may have brought within the limits of feasibility certain public works and the more expensive type of enclosures; and second, that short-run fluctuations in the rate of interest may have contributed to determining the exact timing of some of these activities, particularly in the second half of the eighteenth century when those fluctuations tended to be more violent. The direct relevance of trends in the rate of interest to commerce and industry is less obvious, but the multiplier effect of non-industrial investment activity cannot be ignored. Thus,

> it should suffice at the present preliminary stage of investigation to register the importance of interest rates. . . . For some undertakings there is indeed no obvious clue that it was considered. For others, particularly those at the margin, it was certainly relevant at some stage. . . . It seems safe to say that the rate of interest entered into a significant proportion of decisions to undertake economic activity. (Pressnell, 1960, 210)

The influence of the downward trend in the rate of interest was primarily to stimulate borrowing and investment. It can hardly have acted as a magnet to draw hoardings into the open capital market or to dissuade the wealthy from putting their savings into unproductive stately homes. Yet the fact that the enormously enhanced demand for capital did not lead, except in wartime, to any very serious upward pressure on rates of interest indicates that the new demands were easily met. Thus, the relatively low rate of interest at a time of high demand for capital was not so much the instrument of capital formation, as an indication that the capital already existed and was now being channelled into productive employment.

Whether the new capital came from rent or from the accumulated profits of trade or industry, it was still necessary, if the pace of economic growth was to be accelerated, to direct this capital into productive employment. Much of it, of course, found its way naturally, and almost automatically, into such uses. A landlord sufficiently alert economically to increase his rent income by initiating enclosures would also be one to seize an opportunity of exploiting mineral deposits on his land. Typical of this class was John Christian Curwen of Cumberland, an encloser of commons and a vigorous developer of coalmines.

Landlords were generally (though not invariably) the chief beneficiaries of improved transport facilities, and there was a natural flow of rents into turnpikes, river navigation and canals, which in turn led to higher estate incomes. The greater part of turnpike capital was supplied by landed proprietors, and there were few canal companies in which land-owners were not principal shareholders. Industrial profits most naturally were ploughed back into further industrial investment, while merchants engaged in particular trades, or the trades of a particular region, naturally turned their capital to the industries whose raw materials or finished products they handled. The Weaver and Sankey Brook navigations, for example, the main arteries of the Cheshire salt industry, were largely financed by the Liverpool merchants who handled the trade in salt. These capital flows, however, tend, on the whole, to account for the 'normal' rate of economic growth; they were not susceptible to the sudden augmentation essential for an industrial revolution. For this purpose new channels for capital flow must be dug, new institutions created and new magnets installed to draw capital to where it is most needed.

The most important of the new institutions which opened channels for the flow of capital from its suppliers to its users were the banks. Banking was a development mainly of the eighteenth century. Joint-stock, chartered banks were established first in the capital cities of London and Edinburgh in the 1690s. Two other joint-stock banks followed in Edinburgh in the early eighteenth century, but in England the monopoly of joint-stock banking conferred upon the Bank of England in 1708 restricted banking to partnerships and family concerns throughout the eighteenth century. These small banking houses fell into two groups – the 'London private banks' which originated in the goldsmiths of the seventeenth century, and the 'country banks', the earliest of which emerged in the early eighteenth century, but whose real development occurred after 1760.

In the context of economic development, the banks of the eighteenth century performed two main functions. They oiled the wheels of business by facilitating payments (through their issues of paper money and their remittance business); and they made advances to businessmen and public authorities. Though the former was an exceedingly valuable service and an essential prerequisite of rapid industrialization, the latter is more relevant to the study of capital formation in the eighteenth century.

Banks used their deposits and their powers of credit creation to lend both in the short and the long run. The former was met mainly by the discounting of bills of exchange, and went part of the way towards meeting the businessman's requirements for variable capital. The latter mostly took the form of advances, rather than of direct shareholding, against which the bankers' need for liquidity militated. For this reason, the direct contribution of eighteenth-century bankers to the finance of industry was not substantial, and tended to be confined to certain industries or to businesses with which the banker had a personal connection (some banks developed out of existing industrial or commercial undertakings). Bank lending nevertheless may have played a significant part in the finance of enclosures, of turnpike trust, river navigation and canal companies, and of a wide range of public works. Though, for the most part, the finance of this type of undertaking was a local matter, the banking network, in which the London private bankers acted as links between country bankers in different parts of the country, performed a valuable role in channelling surplus savings to areas of need.

For the system as a whole London provided channels through which capital was transferred from one part of the country to another and a means by which the resources of non-industrial banks were made available to industry. (Pressnell, 1956, 401)

While it is important not to exaggerate their contribution, the banks' role in financing the industrial expansion of the eighteenth century is unmistakable. In the context of the study of the origins of the Industrial Revolution, however, it is no less important to establish a precise chronology of this development, since it is clear that at least some of the financial assistance rendered by banks resulted from the ability of bankers to see opportunities of profitable lending in the economic developments that were already taking place. For at least some of the banking developments of the period of the Industrial Revolution, there is a case for arguing that they were the product of the industrial development, rather than the reverse. The chronology of the growth of the country banks, in particular, makes it difficult to regard the creation of this type of banking facility as a prerequisite to industrial expansion: 'growth became really marked [only] from the 1780s' (Pressnell, 1956, 8). The simultaneous evolution of both banking and industry make it virtually impossible to distinguish cause from effect in the development of either.

The chronological problem, indeed, underlies the whole field of capital formation in the eighteenth century. There is a virtue in trying to distinguish cause from effect, and it is in the nature of a cause to precede an effect; yet there are few aspects of this branch of eighteenth-century economic history which permit the establishment of a chronology precise enough to justify confident assertion as to cause and effect. This is as true of trends in the rate of interest as it is of trends in savings from accumulated rents, lending by country banks or fluctuations in the rate of stately home building. To a limited extent, growth is a self-generating business. The problem with which this book is concerned, however, is the initiation of a fast rate of growth, and in this context it is important to be able to distinguish the 'new' elements in capital formation in the eighteenth century which met the additional net investment necessary for a spurt in the rate of economic growth. According to the analysis of this chapter, these elements would appear to be the growth of profits from increased overseas trade; the progress of the enclosure movement and the growth of population, which, by increasing the yield of land and driving up agricultural prices respectively, raised estate incomes substantially; the diminution of the number of estates coming on to the market which forced the savings of mercantile and industrial tycoons into the capital market; and, possibly, a temporary relaxation in the pace of stately home building. Lower rates of interest in the last two-thirds of the century made it easier for industry, agriculture, transport, building and public works to absorb the capital created or released in these ways, a process which was facilitated by the evolution of banking.

At best, however, an increase in the availability of capital is a trend which permits growth to occur. It is not in itself a cause of growth unless it can be argued that a shortage of capital has previously inhibited growth. Even in this circumstance the increased availability of capital is no more than the removal of a hindrance to growth. And there is little evidence that the British economy before the Industrial Revolution was seriously short of capital: a more likely diagnosis is one of unemployed resources.

> The inducement to invest is limited by the size of the market. . . . It is a matter of common observation that in the poorer countries the use of capital equipment in the production of goods and services for the domestic market is inhibited by the small size of that market, by the lack of domestic purchasing power, not in monetary but in real terms. (Nurkse, 1953, 6)

The significant factor behind the growth of investment in the eighteenth century may conceivably have been the widening of the market for consumer goods rather than increased accumulation of capital. It is not therefore beyond the bounds of possibility that the fall in the rate of interest in the late seventeenth and early eighteenth century was the consequence of a growing surplus of the supply of capital over demand for it. In these circumstances the increased flow of capital which characterized the Industrial Revolution should be regarded as a necessary pre-condition of accelerated growth rather than as a cause of that acceleration.

IV
The Commercial Origins

Other chapters in this book show how, in the main, most explanations of the origins of the Industrial Revolution concentrate on factors concerning the supply of goods and services. Yet, in the circular flow of wealth, demand plays some part. Though no single factor can, in isolation, explain so dramatic a transformation in the means and scale of production as the Industrial Revolution of the eighteenth century, an increased demand could, of itself, be a powerful means of inducing significant changes in the methods of production. Greater demand, leading to higher turnover for manufacturers and merchants, might lead to some economies of scale. More likely it will tend to create some bottlenecks in the chain of production. Sooner or later the resources of inventors and entrepreneurs will be focused on these bottlenecks, and solutions in the form of new techniques, new processes or the utilization of new raw materials may be forthcoming. And the expectation of a steadily growing demand is itself the most favourable environment for innovating entrepreneurship. In 1932 Miss Gilboy suggested that the tendency of the earlier historians of the Industrial Revolution to concentrate on inventions was likely to mislead because it was only a partial approach to the problem, and that until attention was also focused on the demand side of the market equation, a satisfactory explanation was unlikely to emerge.

The demand for industrial products is represented, of course, by both overseas and home markets. So far as the former are concerned, one of the most commonly quoted generalizations is that the Industrial Revolution was the natural consequence of the commercial expansion of the eighteenth century. It is important, however, to distinguish between expanding overseas markets as a growing source of *demand* for the products of manufacturing industry, and the profits of growing trade with these markets as a source for the accumulation of *capital*.

The latter aspect of Britain's expanding commerce has been considered in Chapter III, and for the purpose of this chapter, it is overseas trade as a source of demand which is being considered. And before scrutinizing this aspect of overseas trade more closely, some attempt ought to be made to keep it in proportion. [According to the most reliable estimates of national income in the mid-eighteenth century, exports of British products amounted to only 10–12 per cent of the national product.] Thus, even if export demand were to double in any given period, it would only result in an addition of little more than 10 per cent to the national income. But since exports consisted overwhelmingly of manufactured goods, the growth of overseas markets would have a relatively greater impact on the demand for manufactures.

A further warning is necessary against the tendency to assume that increased income generated through the expansion of overseas trade would automatically be passed on, through a sort of multiplier mechanism, to induce expansion in other related sectors of the economy. As Berrill has shown (1960), there is always a danger of the export sector remaining a mere enclave. This was quite possibly the case to some extent, for example, with the rise of the re-export trade in the eighteenth century. For most of the eighteenth century re-exports accounted for between one-quarter and one-third of the value of total exports. This trade, of course, by-passed the manufacturing sector, and, apart from the employment of shipping, only impinged upon the home economy in any broader way through mercantile profits. These were not infrequently translated into 'stately homes', or other forms of conspicuous consumption. In the case of Scotland, Campbell has argued recently (1964) that, though it was the mercantile sector which grew most rapidly in the eighteenth century, the degree of concentration on the tobacco re-export trade tended to isolate this commercial prosperity from the rather more sluggish industrial and agricultural economy.

These important reservations aside, the expansion of overseas markets remains a development of the utmost significance for the industrial advance of Britain in the eighteenth century. Nor was the expansion of exports wholly concentrated, as is so often assumed, in the later part of the century: there was some important growth during the first two-thirds of the century.

The Schumpeter trade statistics (1960) reveal that the eighteenth-century trade expansion was mainly concentrated in two principal periods: first, between the mid-1730s and 1760, when the value of exports of English produce and manufactures roughly doubled; and, second, between 1785 and 1800, when a similar doubling in value occurred. The first thirty-odd years of the century experienced only the mildest of growth in overseas markets, amounting to little more than 28–30 per cent, or barely 1 per cent per annum. More significantly, the quarter-century between 1760 and 1785 was one of almost complete stagnation in overseas trade. In *per capita* terms, allowing for the growth of population, trade probably fell off absolutely during this period. Though war undoubtedly helps to account for this failure, it is not the whole explanation. A major element was certainly the almost complete cessation of grain exports, which in 1750 had accounted for as much as 20 per cent of all Britain's export earnings. This decline, the result of the increased consumption of grain at home by the growing population, was only partly offset by some increase in the exports of manufactured goods.

As a result of this concentration of export expansion into two relatively short periods, the study of the relationship between export markets and home industries is at least somewhat simplified. Moreover, within each of these two periods, the principal developments are reasonably clear, so that it is possible to generalize with some confidence.

In the first, mid-century period of expansion, it was the growth of colonial markets which principally account for the rise. In this twenty-five-year period, exports to the East Indies multiplied in value $3\frac{1}{2}$-fold, those to the American mainland colonies $2\frac{3}{4}$-fold, while those to the West Indies and Ireland doubled. By 1760, colonial markets, which in 1700 had only taken 15 per cent of the value of English exports, accounted now for 40 per cent. These were captive markets, of course, thanks to the Navigation Laws, and it is doubtful how far British exports would have monopolized them had they been open to the competition of other European exporters. But if they had been open to European competitors, one must also argue that other European colonies would also have been open to British traders.

More important, however, than this mere growth of trade, was the change in the composition of the exports that accompanied it. Davis has pointed out that

colonial trade introduced to English industry the quite new possibility of exporting in great quantities manufactures other than woollen goods, to markets where there was no question of the exchange of manufactures for other manufactures. . . . The process of industrialization in England from the second quarter of the eighteenth century was to an important extent a response to colonial demands for nails, axes, firearms, buckets, coaches, clocks, saddles, handkerchiefs, buttons, cordage and a thousand other things. (Davis, 1962, 290)

Though the value of woollen cloth exported rose by one-third during this twenty-five-year period, the share of non-woollen manufactures rose from 30 per cent of total exports of home produce and manufactures to 45 per cent. The part played by this particular development in stimulating growth in industries such as iron, copper, lead, linen, paper, leather and glass in the mid-century should not therefore be under-estimated.

One market, above all, grew most significantly during the middle decades of the eighteenth century. Ashton first drew attention to the importance of the growth of the Irish market (1960, 11). Between the late 1730s and the late 1760s, trade with Ireland trebled in value. Ireland ceased to be regarded with economic hostility, the Irish market coming to be seen as complementary to the home economy rather than competitive.

> If we consider [wrote a pamphleteer early in the century] how greatly we are already Gainers by the Trade and Industry of that Country, poor as it is, we shall perhaps . . . begin to think that the Wealth and Prosperity of Ireland is not only compatible with that of England, but highly conducive also to its Riches, Grandeur and Power. (Quoted by Davis, 1962, 291)

In the second period of growth, the trade expansion after the Peace of 1783 was extremely narrowly based. Ninety-two per cent of the increase of value of exports of home produce and manufactures by 1800 consisted of increased quantities of only six commodities – cotton cloth, woollen cloth, linen cloth, copper and brass, iron and sugar: 84 per cent of the increase was attributable to only four of these – cotton, wool, copper and brass and iron: and 71 per cent to merely two of them – cotton (accounting for 42 per cent) and wool (29 per cent). So far as total exports were concerned, the French War which began in 1793 quickly increased Britain's entrepot trade. Fifty-seven per cent of the increase in the value of total exports between 1792 and 1800 was provided by re-exports.

Thus, for the trade expansion to have played an effective part in stimulating industrial growth, it would be necessary to show a significant multiplier effect from the expansion of this restricted range of export-based industries. This multiplier effect, by means of which expanding turnover of the industry or industries of Rostow's 'leading sector' stimulated rising incomes in related sectors, would operate through the rising purchases of raw materials, through a growing demand for transport services, through the demand for machinery and other forms of fixed assets, and through the expansion of subsidiary or related industries such as the clothing industry (in the case of cotton and woollen textiles) or nail-making and engineering (in the case of iron).

Certainly there must have been such a multiplier effect to some extent, but the extent can be exaggerated. Habakkuk and Deane have argued (1963, 75–6) that this effect in the cotton and iron industry may have been slighter than is often assumed: the whole of the supply of raw material for the cotton industry, most of it for the linen industry, and a part of it for the woollen industry, was imported, so that the effect of the multiplier backwards through raw material supply in these industries would be limited. To some extent, of course, the greater imports of raw cotton and flax would tend to increase the demand for British exports to the West Indies, America and the Baltic.

There are grounds for supposing, moreover, that the expansion of overseas trade in the last fifteen years of the eighteenth century owed something to the fortuitous circumstances of war. The falling-off of trade during the American War of Independence left exports at a low ebb: exports of English produce and manufactures were lower in 1779–81 than in any years since the early 1740s. Thus, the leap forward in the mid-1780s may be explained at least partly in terms of the backlog of export orders accumulating in markets cut off during the war, not least in the newly independent United States. Without the war, the level of exports would certainly have been higher than it was in, say, 1782 and 1783, and the rate of growth during the mid- and late 1780s would therefore have been less dramatic than it was in the event. The artificially low starting-point in the mid-1780s tends to exaggerate the steepness of the growth curve.

The French wars after 1793 probably did more good than harm to British exporters. Exports to Europe grew much faster than did those to other markets, while British command of the seas enabled her to deny markets to French and French-occupied trading competitors. This was a temporary advantage which Britain could not hope to retain, and, to a considerable extent, did not retain, after 1815. But for twenty-two years Britain enjoyed an unusually privileged position in world trade, and even though the withdrawal of these special circumstances after the Peace of Vienna in 1815 contributed to a particularly severe and prolonged depression in the British economy, the war export boom had lasted long enough for the multiplier side-effects to become permanently built into an expanded economy.

The conclusion of these arguments seems to suggest that the sharpness of the expansion in the last years of the century was induced by some fortuitous and ephemeral circumstances which have tended to lend an exaggerated appearance to both trade and industrial trends of the period. Moreover, the benefits of the commercial expansion in this period were restricted to a very narrow range of industries, and the multiplier effect within these industries was probably less pronounced than appears at first sight.

These conclusions do not, of course, deny the significance of the role of overseas trade in stimulating rapid industrial growth, they simply warn us against allocating too much stress to that role, and remind us of the need to bear other, non-commercial factors in mind. Habakkuk and Deane's carefully considered summary is worth quoting:

> The case for regarding international trade as the crucial factor in British economic growth at this period requires further examination. The precise mechanism by which it became an 'engine of growth' or a 'leading sector' has still to be explored. There seems little doubt, however, than an expansion of the volume of overseas trade was capable of having important multiplier effects on the British economy at the end of the eighteenth century, that it tended to be self-reinforcing (in that imports tended to generate exports and vice versa) and that it provided British entrepreneurs with a means of exploiting advances in productivity both in this country and abroad. (1963, 80)

While, for the purpose of analysing the growth of demand for British manufactured goods during the eighteenth century, it may be sufficient to point to rising demand from certain overseas markets in particular periods, it is important to remember that export markets do not expand in isolation and that growing exports from Britain must have been matched, *pari passu*, by increased imports. Indeed, in the absence, thanks partly to a worldwide system of navigation laws, of any substantial net favourable invisible items in the balance of payments, as well as of any substantial net capital movements during the eighteenth century, it would be possible to argue that Britain's rising exports were a necessary response to the need to meet a rising bill for imports. On the other side of the picture, rising demand from the colonies and foreign countries for British products was only made possible by the steady increase in Britain's demand for their products, particularly in view of the compulsory canalization of the greater part of the colonies' exports to British ports. In its turn, of course, the rise in British imports of colonial produce was related to the general growth of the British economy, so that the growth of colonial markets cannot be regarded as a wholly exogenous stimulus to growth.

Whatever influence is attributed to the growth of overseas demand, the fact remains that for most individual industries. and certainly for all industries put together, home demand predominated and was therefore able to exercise a more decisive influence on output. Though, from its nature, home demand was likely to be less volatile than overseas, quite a small proportionate shift here was likely to matter more than quite a large change overseas.

In broad terms, the significant variables affecting the level of home demand were the level of average real income, the distribution of income and relative shifts of prices between the principal commodity groups. The accurate measurement of change in the level of real wages requires data relating both to money wages and to commodity prices, and in both these fields there is a severe paucity of material for the eighteenth century. There were wide geographical variations in both wages and prices in the eighteenth century, and the temptation to generalize from a limited number of series relating only to one or a few parts of the country can prove extremely misleading.

Up to the present only two useful attempts to measure the progress of real wages in the eighteenth century have been made, and both these have severe limitations. Phelps Brown and Hopkins (1956, 311–14) have related the price of a composite unit of consumer goods to a constructed index of wage rates of building craftsmen in the south of England. Gilboy (1934) has applied an index of prices drawn from some institutional contracts for goods to several series of labourers' and craftsmen's wages in different parts of the country. In spite of many gaps in the time series, the Gilboy figures are the more valuable of these two attempts, since they help to bring out the important regional variations concealed by the single metropolitan index provided by Phelps Brown and Hopkins. Both indices may be criticized on various technical grounds, but beggars cannot be choosers, and, in the absence of a wider selection of the kind of price data desirable for this purpose, these tables offer the best guide currently available. Conclusions drawn from them must, it goes without saying, be tentative in the extreme.

Some of the trends that emerge from a study of these figures are insignificant enough to be discounted largely, if not wholly, by the margin of error implicit in the data. The Phelps Brown index, for example, indicates a modest rise in real income during the second quarter of the eighteenth century, with the level of the early part of the century sharply restored by the price rise of the Seven Years' War. Thereafter, apart from some not very significant short-run fluctuations associated with wars, this index indicates a remarkable stability throughout the last forty years of the century. Similarly, the Gilboy material for the south of England also suggests a very slight rise during the 1720s and 1730s, a gain which was also lost in the '50s and '60s. This index shows a continuing slight downward trend for labourers in the south of England for the rest of the century. But the long-term movements revealed in both instances are very slight.

Much more significant trends were revealed by the Gilboy data for real wages in the north of England. Here, the rise in the early part of the century was much more marked – gains of up to 45 per cent being registered for the first forty years of the century. These gains were only reduced, not eliminated, by the price rises of the middle decades, and continued through the later decades of the century. Such data as are available for Scotland (Hamilton, 1963, 351–7) indicate even more steeply rising real wages. It is very probable that more rapidly rising prices began to overtake the money wages of most groups in most regions in the last decade of the century (Gayer, Rostow and Schwartz, 1953, II, 657).

This great and extremely significant disparity between regional trends was the product, first, of the very substantial differential existing between the two regions at the beginning of the century, wages in the north of England being, in some instances, barely half of those in the south; and, second, of the progress of industrialization in the north of England during the century, which demanded the magnet of higher wages to attract labour into industry in an area hitherto relatively sparsely populated. But it is worth bearing in mind that if this significant rise in real wages in the north of England is to be explained in terms of growing industrialization in those parts it will not be permissible to reverse the argument, and to explain the expansion of industry in terms of rising home demand. The two developments were, of course, inextricably interwoven, and the allocation of precedence becomes extremely hazardous.

So far as the demand for the products of industry is concerned, these trends, of course, tell only part of the story. They are limited to the wage-earning population, and only cover that extremely imperfectly. There were also wide sections of the population who may be broadly described as the upper and middle classes, the owner-occupying farmers, and a wide range of self-employed workers in industry, transport and commerce. For the levels of consumption of these social groups virtually no information is available. Statistically, the only approach to their real incomes is a comparison of the trends in average real output with those of the real wages just discussed, and the rough-and-ready nature of this method of measurement will mean that only the most decisive shifts can be accepted as reasonable indications of trends. Deane and Cole (1962, 78) have made an attempt to measure total and average real output decennially throughout the eighteenth century, and though their figures must be subject to a wide range of possible errors, not least from our ignorance of the course of population change before the nineteenth century, the trends indicated by their figures do seem to make some sense in relation to other developments.

This estimate of average real output indicates a very slow rise to about 1760, in the course of which there was an addition of about one-fifth to output per head in real terms. This increase was achieved fairly steadily and showed only a very slight tendency to accelerate. For the next twenty years or so there was a setback, and the 1780 level was no higher than that of 1760, or, if the government sector is omitted (which tended to fluctuate rather violently owing to the sudden heavy augmentation of expenditure in wartime), than that of 1750. After 1780, real output per head rose sharply, almost 30 per cent being added in the last twenty years of the century.

The rise in the first half of the century, of a very modest nature, must relate fairly closely to the gains in real wages. While output rose faster than wages in the south, it fell behind the increase of wages in the north. Thus, although there was obviously some fairly substantial redistribution of income *geographically* during this period, there does not appear to have been sufficient discrepancy between these two indices to indicate any serious redistribution of income *socially*. In the last two decades, however, and particularly in the 1790s, average real output grew appreciably faster than most real wages in all parts of the country, suggesting some significant redistribution in favour of the non-wage-earning class. A part of this redistribution is to be accounted for by the disproportionately fast rise of landowners' incomes already referred to (see p. 47 above), but much of it must have taken the form of rapidly rising middle-class incomes. Middle-class incomes also benefited from this redistribution, and the English middle class was numerous.

English society at the end of the seventeenth century was distinguished from the societies of the continent by the large part of the
national income which accrued to people with moderate sized incomes – according to Gregory King, as much as half. The relatively
great importance of this middle group is due, in turn, partly to social
causes of long standing, and partly to differences of tax systems. The
middle-income groups were relatively large in England for the same
reasons as they were relatively large in all the great trading centres of
the pre-industrial age. . . . Moreover, this large middle market was a
market for solid substantial goods as opposed to fine quality goods,
i.e. for just the sort of goods suitable for machine production.
(Habakkuk, 1955, 154)

The middle classes were likely to have had a high income elasticity of
demand for the products of the major consumer goods industries –
cotton goods, pottery, glass and many branches of metal-ware.

The income elasticity of demand for textile goods must have been
fairly high at the time, and it is quite likely that rising agricultural
productivity and incomes at home furnished the spur to the expansion of the cotton textile trade and to the innovational activity which
characterised it. Price elasticities, too, must have been high so long as
it was largely a question of displacing Indian imports. (Ohlin,
1959, 346)

This redistribution of income is unlikely to have involved any long-
term loss of real income by any group: it was achieved as a result of the
substantial growth of real product which left the country half as
wealthy again per head at the end of the century compared with the
beginning. Deane has summed up this redistribution as follows:

Within the limits of the comparison that can be made, however,
some suggestive results emerge. It would appear, for example, that
there had been a marked increase in the inequality of incomes
between 1688 and 1812, as shown by the corresponding estimates of
average incomes per head. The 'upper classes', in general, seem to
have expanded their incomes by more than the national average, and
the small farmers, the unskilled labourers, and the poor seem to have
. . . increased their standard of living by less than the average.
(Deane, 1955–6, 37)

At present, too few price series relating to the eighteenth century are available to permit any confident and reliable generalization regarding shifts in consumption patterns. Some play has been made from time to time of the significance of a period of relatively low grain prices between about 1720 and 1750. These 'increased corn wages,' observed Malthus, 'instead of occasioning an increase of population exclusively, were so expended as to occasion a decided elevation in the standard of their comforts and conveniences'. Since this was, in any case, a period of slowly rising real wages, the added bounty of low food prices, in other words, would have permitted a very real increase in the consumption of manufactured goods. Statistically, however, this period of low food prices seems to rest on very slender foundations. It rests, in fact, on the trends indicated by three series of wheat prices, in Exeter, Winchester and Eton, the last two being institutional, contract prices. These three indices agree roughly in showing a level of grain prices in the 1730s and '40s about 15 per cent lower than the average for the preceding thirty years.

But evidence from other parts of the country (Mitchison, 1965) suggests that generalizations drawn from such narrow sources may be misleading. There is a strong possibility at least that, when sufficient evidence has been assembled, this 'period of low food prices' may turn out to be relatively insignificant – that the dip in prices, in general, for the whole country, may be insufficient to stand the weight of argument which has been erected upon it. It may be worth noting in this context that, in contrast, the period of most rapid economic growth in the last two decades of the century were characterized by the erosion of the purchasing power of the masses as food prices rose more rapidly than wages.

It seems unlikely, then, that there were any very dramatic shifts in the field of home demand during the eighteenth century, though the possibility of some marginal shifts playing a subsidiary role in stimulating increased production should not be ruled out. Moreover, since the sharp increase in output we know as the Industrial Revolution occurred at a fairly precise moment in time, the timing of the expansion of home demand is a matter of some importance. For the bulk of the population in the south of England, most of the gains for consumption seem to have accrued during the first half of the century, and cannot therefore go very far towards explaining the great industrial leap forward in the 1780s. So far as wage-earners in the North and in Scotland were concerned, the substantial gain in purchasing power seems to have been fairly evenly distributed over the whole century, and certainly does not show any marked concentration in, say, the last third of the century which would help to explain a sudden spurt in industrial production. Only the redistribution of income in favour of the middle and upper classes, which was a marked feature of the last twenty years of the century, can be said to have a sufficiently close chronological correlation to justify linking it causally with the most rapid rise in industrial production.

The picture of the role played by markets in stimulating an industrial revolution can only be completed by linking together the trends both at home and overseas. During the first four decades of the century, the strongest stimulus to production came from the rising incomes of the population in the north of England and Scotland. But, since Scotland and England north of the Trent probably contained little more than one-third of the total population, the effects of the substantial growth of purchasing power in these parts should not be exaggerated. The rise in real wages began from such extremely low levels that, in any case, it is likely that a considerable proportion of the marginal additions to income would be expended on additional food rather than on manu-factured goods. During the same period overseas demand was only growing at an extremely moderate rate. Thus, while the growth of demand was persistent enough to drive the economy slowly and steadily ahead during the first few decades of the eighteenth century, at no time was this pressure sufficiently dramatic to lead to a major spurt in industrial production.

The absence of any really significant quantitative developments during this period should not be allowed to obscure some important qualitative changes in the nature of this slowly growing demand. Even if, as yet, the labourer of the north of England and Scotland was buy-ing little in the way of manufactured goods, his rising real income was slowly leading him into the market for this type of expenditure. His marginal propensity to consume manufactured goods may initially have been slight, but it could rise sharply. While in the early or even the middle decades of the century this source of mass demand may have remained largely potential, rather than actual, it augured much for the future if rising incomes could be sustained. And overseas, the significant development was less the overall expansion of trade, or even the growth of colonial markets, than the growing diversification of British exports: the agelong dependence upon woollen cloth was being broken down and the other textiles, metal goods and miscellaneous manu-factures were beginning to capture a widening share of the market.

No longer was Britain to be a country with a single export industry.

In terms of an expanding industrial sector, this diversification of exports was to prove a factor of major importance in the 1750s and '60s when, as we have seen earlier, the rate of growth of real wages began to fall off. The lag in home demand was compensated – possibly more than compensated – by the sharp rise in exports which had begun a little earlier, in the 1740s. This complementary growth of overseas trade prevented the steady expansion of industrial production from being interrupted by the levelling-off of real wages.

At the end of the Seven Years' War, the position was reversed. Foreign trade stagnated, while the renewed advance of real wages once again sustained aggregate demand. And when, by the 1780s, rising prices eroded the gains of the continued rise in money wages, the revival of overseas trade kept the ball rolling. As the 1780s passed into the 1790s, buoyant overseas markets were joined by increasing middle- and upper-class purchasing power as rising prices bit into working-class incomes and initiated the profit inflation of the war period. From 1793 onwards windfalls, in the shape of new overseas markets and the sharp increase in government war expenditure, added yet a further stimulus to industrial production.

There was, in short, a fairly persistent pull from demand for most of the century. Its source varied, coming at one time from abroad, at another time from at home. When from the home market, it originated first from one class, then from another; now from one region, now from another. The combined pressure from all sources of demand seems to have been remarkably steady throughout most of the first eight decades of the century, though it is just possible that the overlapping of an export boom in the 1740s with a period of continued growth in real wages steepened the growth curve slightly during that decade. The last twenty years of the century witnessed more rapidly accelerating demand from several sectors to an extent that transformed the whole character of both home and overseas trade in a very brief period.

Thus, in both these sharply delineated periods, demand may have played an important part in shaping the character of industrial change, first, during the greater part of the century, in sustaining *some* growth in real terms, and, second, in the period of the 'take-off' in providing a key sector of expansion.

V

The Social and Intellectual Origins

For a long time many historians were prepared to give technology a central place in their interpretations of the Industrial Revolution, and, even today, when a monolithic interpretation is less fashionable, few are ready to reject the role of technological advance completely. The greater reluctance nowadays to give pride of place to technological change arises from observation of its failure, unaided, to promote growth in underdeveloped countries. The most advanced technologies are generally available to any country wishing to employ them, yet the great majority of countries remain backward because they do not employ them. They do not employ them not because they do not know about them or lack access to the relevant information, but because they lack the capital to implement them, the technical skill to operate and maintain them or, more fundamentally, the willingness to accept the social disruption which inevitably accompanies them, and the entre-preneurial drive to employ them on a large scale.

There may, therefore, be no necessary correlation between advances in technology and economic growth. Nonetheless, given the capital, skill and desire for growth essential to the employment of new tech-niques, technological innovation must remain an important factor in particular phases of the economic advance of nations. In broad terms, technological developments facilitate economic growth by reducing the cost of producing a good or service. (This involves increasing the productivity of a factor of production – land, labour or capital – and permits, say, the production of two shirts for the price of a single shirt formerly.) This reduction in cost may be achieved by making available to industry a raw material hitherto inaccessible or unusable (e.g. coke for iron smelting, or cotton for textile fabrics). These processes assist in overcoming the tendency in a growing economy for marginal costs to rise, one of the most intractable barriers to permanent economic advance. Some of the new techniques employed at the time of the Industrial Revolution in Britain had dramatic consequences of these kinds: the inventions in cotton spinning resulted in the successive reduction of the price of cotton yarn from 38s per lb in 1786 to 2s 11d in 1832; Darby's and Cort's inventions, by freeing the ironmaster from the threat of rising marginal costs of charcoal, and by raising the productivity of both labour and capital in the process, brought down the price of a ton of bar iron from about £18 per ton in the middle of the century to about £8 in the early 1820s; and the Duke of Bridgewater's first canal reduced the delivered price of coal in Manchester overnight from eightpence a hundredweight to fourpence. By shifting supply curves to the right (i.e. allowing producers to market a greater quantity at the same price, or the same quantity at a lower price), real purchasing power was increased.

To explain growth, however, it is insufficient merely to draw attention to the availability of new techniques of production. There must, in the first instance, be a readiness to put the new techniques promptly and effectively to work. There must, in other words, be entrepreneurs as well as inventors. The work of inventors is commonly available (though perhaps after a short delay imposed by patent laws or by the problems of the dissemination of scientific or technological information) without regard to geographical, economic or political frontiers. The product of entrepreneurial activity, on the other hand, at least before the days of widespread international investment, is mostly effective only within a national economy. While both these elements – technological and entrepreneurial – are important for growth, they do not necessarily coexist. Nevertheless, the aim of this chapter will be to suggest not only that they did coexist in Britain in the eighteenth century but also that their coexistence owed something to a set of common origins.

The handful of key inventions which are usually cited in connection with the Industrial Revolution are not in themselves proof of an increase in the rate of technological innovation. However, the statistics of inventions in the eighteenth century (as measured by the issue of patents of invention) are sufficiently unequivocal:

The development of invention is reflected in the tables of the Commissioners of Patents. Before the 1760s the number of patents granted in any single year rarely exceeded a dozen, but in 1766 it rose abruptly to 31, and in 1769 to 36. For some years the average remained below this figure, but in 1783 there was a sudden jump to 64. Thereafter the number fell, until in 1792 another bound brought it to 85. During the next eight years it fluctuated about a mean of 67, but from 1798 an upward movement brought it to a peak of 107 in 1802. Other pinnacles appeared in 1813 and 1818, but these were not outstanding. In 1824, however, the number of patents shot up suddenly once more – to 180 – and in the following year of boom it attained the unprecedented height of 250. (Ashton, 1948, 90)

To some extent the increase in the annual issue of patents may be explained in terms of increasing resort by inventors to the Patent Office: some of the earlier inventors (Abraham Darby, for example), for one reason or another, did not take out patents for all their inventions. Moreover, many of the patents issued during the period of the Industrial Revolution were inevitably for processes which made relatively trifling contributions to economic growth. The really important inventions were relatively few in number. On the other hand, it has been claimed that, under the influence of 'more rigorous rules for the submission of definite specifications, drawings, and models in order to secure valid patent rights', trivial inventions accounted for a decreasing proportion of patents issued during the eighteenth century. 'The later patents', moreover, 'in contrast with those issued before the middle of the eighteenth century, put the emphasis on the invention of new machines rather than on the introduction of new industries'; while 'in the later period a smaller proportion of the patentees were foreigners' (Bowden, 1925, 14).

There is, without doubt, a correlation between the availability of new processes in the fields of textile manufacture, ironmaking and steam power, and new, higher levels of the annual number of patents. From whatever angle technological developments in the eighteenth century are scrutinized, and making all possible allowances for the complexity of the process of innovation and the sheer difficulty of statistical measurement, there remains fairly convincing evidence of some acceleration in the rate of invention and innovation in the second half of the century. If there was such an acceleration, why did it occur?

Two basic approaches have been made to this problem. The first involves a general theory of inventions which may then be applied to the British experience in the eighteenth century. The second examines the particular circumstances of eighteenth-century Britain.

Theoretical discussion of invention has crystallized around two fundamental approaches – the 'systematic', and the 'heroic'. The former school of thought sees invention as the culmination of a regular process.

71

Usher, for example, observed four stages in this process. In the first, 'the perception of the problem', the need for a new process is consciously noted. In the second, 'the setting of the stage', 'some fortuitous configuration in events or in thought' present to the inventor 'all the data essential to a solution'. The third stage is an 'act of insight by which the essential solution of the problem is found', while the final stage is devoted to 'critical revision and full mastery of the new pattern' (Usher, 1954, 65–6). This pattern of development is generally applicable to all technological situations: 'the succession of events is orderly and logical, and discloses patterns' (Usher, 1954, 79). As with all theories involving stages, however, the time lag between the stages is highly elastic but crucial. The first patent for a coal or coke smelting process in the manufacture of iron was in the year 1589: the first successful invention was that of Darby in the early eighteenth century. Arkwright's successful water-frame for textile spinning was patented in 1769, but it was largely anticipated in most of its essential details in Lewis Paul's near miss of 1738, which, in its turn, came at the end of a long succession of unsuccessful attempts to solve the same problem. The stage was set, in Usher's terms, for the invention of a steam engine already in classical times, so that the hiatus before the third stage of 'fortuitous configuration in thought' lasted for nearly two thousand years. Time lags of such infinite elasticity can make nonsense of the best of theories.

Another variant of the 'systematic' approach is to see technological advance as an inevitable progression in which technical needs set in motion a long chain of social and cultural responses. This view is supported by the simultaneous duplication of some inventions and the 'functional equivalence' of others. When the same process, or one which meets the same technological requirements, appears in different countries, or different parts of the same country, at about the same time, some plausibility is lent to the suggestion that the solution to the particular technological problem has been inevitably evolved as a product of some beneficent cultural metabolism.

> The only possible explanation is some larger, probably social, forces behind, whether we understand them or not, that bring forth not only one but several solutions when the need and broad opportunity for the invention arrives. (Gilfillan, 1945, 72)

This suggestion, in spite of its failure to explain the precise nature of the social process concerned, may have some validity in instances where duplication or equivalence is involved. But many of the key inventions on which the Industrial Revolution was based do not fall into these categories. There were no successful rivals or near equivalents to Darby's coke smelting process, Watt's separate condenser, Dundonald's mineral alkali or Cartwright's power loom, to mention just a few. These were all solutions to technological problems which had teased the best minds for centuries: the timing of these isolated discoveries is all-important.

Nor can it always, or even often, be said that the successful inventor was standing on the shoulders of his less successful predecessors. Many of the most important inventions owed little or nothing to the previous unsuccessful attempts to solve the same problems, except in the purely negative sense that the early failures had shown certain approaches to be fruitless.

Recognizing this difficulty, Usher introduced an additional element which effectively links his theory with the 'heroic' school. It is the greatness of the individual inventor, he said, which determines the timing of the discovery. 'The very superior person does not accomplish things that would never be done by another; he achieves results sooner than persons of less capacity would achieve them.' But, nonetheless, he insists on giving priority to the force of his pattern over the role of the individual: 'It is an error to assume that any given individual is uniquely necessary' (Usher, 1954, 79).

In contrast to this attempt to systematize the process of invention, the 'heroic' school of thought insists on a far greater random element. extending in the process the very restricted role allocated by Usher to the individual inventor. This shift of emphasis results from the focusing of attention on the question of timing.

Timing here is of the essence of the matter. If invention is a con-tinuing process, any loss of time is a permanent loss, the whole course of technical progress is set back permanently, the time lost is never made up. But, in fact, individuals have made a permanent impress on the shape of things. It is true that the rapid advances in the past 150 years seem to give meaning to such phrases as 'the march of science', 'the march of technology', and to create the impression of move-ments pressed along by forces independent of the will, the decisions, the struggles of individuals. In that period one genius trod closely upon the heels of another. But to describe an epoch especially rich in outstanding inventors as one in which individual contribution can no longer be identified is a curious inversion of facts, and as great a misapprehension as it would be to talk of the 'march of painting' in the Netherlands, or the 'march of drama' in the England of the sixteenth and seventeenth centuries. (Jewkes, 1958, 16–17)

While this view rejects any systematic or evolutionary theory of inventions, it puts little back in its place: given the fact of an acceleration in the rate of invention in the later eighteenth century, it begs the question of why more inventors appeared in this period. It can hardly have been simply a function of the growing population.

The special problem of the eighteenth century is therefore not so much explaining the timing of a particular key invention, as explaining why inventions, in general, became more frequent. Abraham Darby solved his particular problem early in the century: it could conceivably have been solved one hundred years before, or after. What really calls for explanation is not the location of the solution to this particular problem in the early eighteenth rather than the early seventeenth or early nineteenth centuries, but why coke smelting was invented broadly in the same period as machine spinning and weaving, steam power, mineral alkali, puddling and rolling.

The interdependence of industries went some way towards accounting for this simultaneity:

So far the process of invention has been traced first in one industry and then in another. The arrangement has the merit of making clear what was involved in each successive step, but it fails to bring out the way in which discoveries in different fields of activity were linked together. Sometimes it was a simple case of imitation, as when the principle of attenuating material by passing it through rollers was transferred from the iron to the textile industry, or when Wilkinson's method of boring cannon was turned to the making of steam-engine cylinders. Sometimes an advance in one sphere was a condition of progress in another, as when the development of coke ovens made possible the extraction of tar. Often two or more industries went hand in hand, each contributing to the forward movement of the other. Without the discovery of smelting with coke, which made it possible to supply larger and more intricate castings, Newcomen could not have perfected his engine; and without Newcomen's engine Darby could hardly have obtained the blast that was necessary to produce iron on the scale required. Both the atmospheric and the steam engine helped to increase the output of coal and metals, and the larger supply of these (and especially of copper and brass) reacted on

the development of engineering. 'Invention is the mother of necessity': an improvement in one process frequently put pressure on those
concerned with an earlier, parallel or later process in the same
industry. (Ashton, 1948, 88–9)

Here again, then, is another explanation which helps to account for
some of the inventions – those that depended upon others—but which
still leaves a great many key inventions not accounted for.

These speculations on the nature and pattern of invention do not,
therefore, amount to a wholly satisfactory explanation of the acceleration in the flow of inventions in late eighteenth-century Britain. Where
general theories fail, as they so often do in social and economic fields,
can any light be thrown on this problem by an examination of the
cultural background of the age?

Clearly the cultural background is of the utmost importance.

A far larger proportion of the adult population is today, for example,
possessed of mathematical, scientific, and engineering knowledge,
and ability to use it, than three hundred, or even thirty years ago.
(Epstein, 1926, 248)

Of course, only a very small proportion of those with access to the relevant technological or scientific knowledge at any point in time will
actually turn their minds to invention, but the number of inventors
must be, to some extent, a function of the breadth of technological
culture in society. And the cultural ·frontiers in society can shift
markedly over time.

The material culture three hundred years ago was very different
from what it is now. It has changed rapidly. And the elements of the
material culture at any one time have a good deal to do with determining the nature of the particular inventions that are made. (Ogburn
and Thomas, 1922, 87)

A new-found interest in scientific discovery was a major feature of
the sixteenth and seventeenth centuries. In Britain this had culminated
in the establishment, in 1660, of the Royal Society, which did much to
guide and intensify what had hitherto been rather random and mis-
directed scientific enquiry. In its early years, in particular, the Royal
Society consciously directed its efforts towards the solution of technological problems in contemporary industry. Yet it is difficult to
substantiate any direct connection between the kind of scientific work

pursued by the members of the Royal Society and the major technological advances of a long period after 1660. For many decades, for example, some of its most brilliant members engaged themselves in the quest for steam power; but, in the event, Newcomen's solution to the problem of the utilization of atmospheric pressure in a steam pump apparently owed nothing at all to the work on steam power simultaneously, if spasmodically and quite fruitlessly in progress in London. The success of Abraham Darby was a triumph of empiricism, not of scientific metallurgy; while the important textile inventions from Kay and Paul in the 1730s onwards fell into the category of artful mechanical contrivance rather than of the application of predetermined physical laws.

Recognizing the existence of an as yet unbridged gap between science and technology, in 1754 a group of enthusiasts created the Royal Society of Arts with a view to providing a much more direct stimulus to industrial and agricultural technology than was currently being given by the Royal Society. The Society of Arts raised quite substantial sums of money which were then offered as prizes for solutions to specific technological problems. The Society's historians claim a very real contribution to economic development:

> In the first twenty-two years of the Society's existence, £16,625 was expended in premiums. But what was their actual influence in other than monetary terms? Four claims can be asserted with confidence. First, they resulted in the reafforestation of very considerable areas of land. Secondly, they played a predominant part in the earlier stages of the 'agricultural revolution', being the means of introducing several new crops to this country and to the colonies and of the invention of new agricultural implements. Thirdly, they fostered the skill of draughtsmanship. And, fourthly, by stimulating the invention of many mechanical devices, they contributed largely to the progress of the Industrial Revolution. (Hudson and Luckhurst, 1954, 16)

Though some inventions of secondary importance owe their origin to competitions organized by the Society of Arts, very few of the really important inventors of the eighteenth century had any contact with the Society.

From time to time Parliament, too, made substantial awards to inventors in recognition of their services to the nation. Thomas Lombe and Edmund Cartwright were both rewarded in this way for their contributions to textile technology. But though inventors may have been aware of the possibility of such rewards coming their way, the grants were too few and too arbitrary for them to be considered as real incentives to invention. In the industrial field, therefore, the inventions fostered by the Society of Arts or rewarded by Parliament were of marginal importance only, and there is a strong case for arguing that industrial technology and scientific research proceeded on independent if parallel lines for a century or possibly more after the foundation of the Royal Society.

In the last third of the eighteenth century, however, the line between these two related fields became more blurred as their interdependence was more firmly established. James Watt's vital developments of Newcomen's steam pump were securely based on laboratory work pursued over a long period in close collaboration with Joseph Black, Professor of Chemistry at Glasgow University, and other academic scientists. Important developments in the chemical industry and glassmaking were closely related to theoretical work in the chemical and physical sciences. Industrialists became more numerous who were either professionally qualified in science – graduates of the Scottish universities – or active in amateur scientific circles. The Lunar Society of the Midlands was unique only in the calibre of its members: comparable groups were banding together in philosophical and debating societies in a great many provincial centres at the same period.

> There was a widespread interest in applied science in the late eighteenth century. Many scientists or 'natural philosophers' had industrial interests, and many industrialists were interested in science. . . . There seems little doubt that such knowledge contributed to the industrial changes of that period. (Musson and Robinson, 1960, 243–4)

Some care, however, is needed in tracing the chronology of cause and effect in these fields. While there can be little doubt that much of the scientific and technological work done by both scientists and industrialists in the late eighteenth century contributed notably to the advance of industry, it is important also to recognize that much of it was itself the product of industrial progress. Thus, while it makes sense to talk of the scientific contribution to the *progress* of the Industrial Revolution, it is less easy to determine the role of science in its *origins*. Progress in industrial technology is self-sustaining: scientific and industrial development were inextricably interwoven in the period of the Industrial Revolution. But where cause was so closely bound up with effect there can be little certainty in the allocation of chronological priorities: growth cannot be satisfactorily explained in terms of itself.

Other efforts have been made to explain the spate of technological innovations in terms of economic pressures. Unlike many Continental countries whose economic development was hindered by frequent and disastrous wars, the economic history of Britain in the two or three centuries before the Industrial Revolution was one of persistent growth, though the rate may seldom have been fast, and was sometimes negligible. And in an island economy with fixed resources of land and minerals, growth must necessarily, sooner or later, disturb a given equilibrium between supply and demand for some of these resources. The consequent rising prices in turn become the incentives for technological changes aimed at permitting producers to substitute different (and, of course, cheaper) raw materials for the traditional, increasingly scarce and dear ones, to economize in their use or to reduce the factor costs of working them up. According to this reasoning, the faster the rate of economic growth, the greater the stimulus to technological advance. The classical examples of this process are the switch from charcoal to coke smelting, and the substitution of machine for hand spinning, both accomplished during the eighteenth century.

Bairoch (1963), who has pressed this analysis most closely, has linked these two particular technological developments together to illustrate a common origin in the improvements in agriculture in the first half of the eighteenth century. Without indicating very specifically just what form they took, Bairoch argued that agricultural improvements in the early eighteenth century produced two main effects of direct consequence to industry. On the one hand, greater agricultural activity created directly an increased demand for ironware in the form of horseshoes. iron for ploughs and other agricultural implements, and nails for new farm buildings, etc., while, on the other, the resultant higher level of agricultural incomes led, thanks to a high income elasticity of demand, to a disproportionate increase in the demand for textile products. It was this unprecedented growth in demand which livened the search for solutions to the technical problems of smelting and spinning, and which therefore led directly to the inventions that made further large-scale expansion possible.

This type of explanation, linking cause and effect in a fairly limited time scale, tends nevertheless also to founder on the rock of chronology. While it is true that, in the mid-eighteenth century, coke smelting was cheaper per ton of pig iron than charcoal smelting, and that machine spinning would have made far more economical use of labour than hand spinning, the relative cost advantage of the more efficient method would also have been true, and was seen to be true, in earlier centuries. The pressure to invent an iron smelting process employing a mineral fuel, exerted through the obvious economic advantages of coal over wood, was present for well over a century before the breakthrough was achieved. The whole cycle from the first awareness of the cost advantage of coal in the late sixteenth century to the final general adoption of coke smelting in the third quarter of the eighteenth century occupied nearly two hundred years. Nor is there much evidence that the pressure was becoming more intensive in the period immediately preceding Darby's discovery, or even in the period preceding the general adoption of coke smelting. Much the same difficulties apply to the spinning industry. While there is little doubt that the economic pressure for the solution of certain technological problems was intensifying during the first half of the eighteenth century, it must remain extremely difficult to show that this tendency played much part in expediting the crucial discoveries.

There is, therefore, a wide range of possible explanations, both theoretical and empirical, of the acceleration in the rate of technological innovation in the late eighteenth century. Few of them satisfy entirely, but, equally, few are wholly devoid of plausibility. Together, since they are not mutually exclusive, they may add up to a useful contribution to the solution of this problem. A final discussion of the problem, however, must wait until we have examined the other aspect of innovation in the late eighteenth century – the increase in the willingness of society to put the new techniques quickly and effectively to work in productive industry.

This was the function of entrepreneurs. The entrepreneur organized production. He it was who brought together the capital (his own or somebody else's) and the labour force, selected the most appropriate site for operations, chose the particular techniques of production to be employed, bargained for the raw materials and found outlets for the finished product.

I would hazard the speculation that if we ever did the research necessary to get some crude idea of the magnitudes involved, we would discover that improved economic organization was as important as technological change in the development of the Western world between 1500 and 1830. (North, 1965, 87–8)

Some of the changes in the organization of production, like the substitution of factories for domestic production in the textile industries, were the direct result of the employment of new techniques: in these cases the rise in productivity clearly stemmed from technological rather than organizational changes. Moreover, so far as business organization in the eighteenth century was concerned, except in the field of transport, where the capital requirements were larger and there were particular problems in connection with the purchase of land, there were no new developments. The joint stock company, where it had not actually been proscribed by the Bubble Act of 1720, continued to be exceptional in industry. Until well into the nineteenth century the one-man business or the small partnership predominated in British industry. This meant, inevitably, that the greater number of industrial firms were ephemeral.

In many cases, of course, the individual entrepreneur was also the inventor: most of the inventors of the new industrial processes which contributed to the Industrial Revolution attempted to exploit their own inventions. Some, like Darby, Arkwright and Watt, did so with outstanding success; others – Cartwright, Cort and Hargreaves come to mind – discovered that entrepreneurial qualities were not necessarily linked with inventive capacity. But for the economy as a whole to take advantage of new techniques it needed more than the exploitation of a new process by its inventor.

The very idea of an industrial revolution implies the adoption of new methods of production on a vast scale. Not only, in other words, is the multiplication of entrepreneurial units essential: it is this very duplication of effort which often plays the major role in perfecting the original invention. Thus, though there is a place for the inventor-entrepreneur, most of what is involved in an industrial revolution can only be carried through by a multiplicity of entrepreneurs. For every new invention there must have been, one may say, a score, or a hundred, of new entrepreneurs. These new entrepreneurs may have lacked the spark of creative genius that stamps the inventor, but they must have had all the other characteristics of personality that go to create the successful entrepreneur. Because they were imitators or opportunists rather than innovators, posterity has seldom honoured this class of man; yet for every Arkwright in the Industrial Revolution there were a hundred such anonymous, busy, tireless, profit-seeking employers.

If the particular personal qualities that made a successful entrepreneur were present in a constant proportion of the population, entrepreneurs would, of course, increase in proportion as population grew.

Moreover, the steady, modest growth which, as we have seen, was a feature of most of the first three-quarters of the eighteenth century, would create additional opportunities for entrepreneurs. Growth in the number of entrepreneurs in this way would, nevertheless, remain a function of a moderate rate of growth. In contrast, the Industrial Revolution of the last quarter of the eighteenth century could only have occurred as a consequence of an explosion in the number of potential entrepreneurs in British society.

Apart from the occasional coincidence of inventor and entrepreneur in the same individual, there are other respects in which inventors and entrepreneurs drew upon similar resources of personality, and which permit the two roles to be studied here jointly. Both types, for example, are individualists; they display a high awareness of future possibilities; they are non-conservative in the sense of having a particular interest in novelty and innovation; they possess more than average energy; and they both strive for the satisfaction of success or achievement. There was a degree, therefore, of joint supply of entrepreneurs and inventors, and assuming there to have been an increase in their numbers (and possibly, quality) in the eighteenth century, the problem is to explain why this should have occurred, and why it occurred when it did.

It is necessary to repeat at the start a generalization which has been made in varying forms in many other places in this book already. This is to the effect that explanations of an increase in the numbers of inventors and entrepreneurs in terms of previous economic growth must be inadequate. In searching for the origins of a phenomenon like the Industrial Revolution we are dealing with a major discontinuity in history. Its origins are more likely to lie in other, exogenous, possibly non-economic discontinuities. Steady, moderate economic growth may, given appropriate circumstances, generate and sustain continued, moderate growth: it is unlikely (and it is over-optimistic of historians to expect it) to transmute itself through some mysterious alchemy into the explosion of an industrial revolution. Thus, the spurt in all forms of innovational activity must necessarily be explained in some other, possibly non-economic, discontinuity in eighteenth-century (or, conceivably, seventeenth-century) history.

Ever since Weber (1904-5) postulated a causal linkage between what he called the 'protestant ethic' and the 'spirit of capitalism', attempts have been made to associate various phases of the economic development of the Protestant world with the peculiar doctrinal teachings of these churches. Since much of this discussion has been centred on the discontinuity produced by the Reformation, this approach is to some extent irrelevant to the study of the Industrial Revolution. However, in the 1920s, Tawney's contribution to this debate (1926) shifted the chronological emphasis in a way that brought the discussion nearer to the Industrial Revolution.

The decisive change in relation to the spread of capitalist endeavour was not, according to Tawney, the Protestant break with Rome in the early sixteenth century, but the appearance of the Puritan sects in the later sixteenth and seventeenth centuries. Though Puritanism was an important element in English history from the later decades of the reign of Elizabeth, it was not until the Restoration of 1660 that the extreme Protestant sects emerged as clearly defined minorities. Moreover, it was after 1660 that members of these sects – Quakers, Congregationalists, Baptists, Presbyterians and Unitarians – begin noticeably to occupy a disproportionately large place in the ranks of the entrepreneurs. A survey of a fairly random selection of principal entrepreneurs and inventors of the Industrial Revolution period shows that, of those whose religious affiliations could be traced, 49 per cent were non-conformists (Hagen, 1964, 305–8). In contrast, in the 1770s, there were only about 1,250 Dissenting congregations in England and Wales, and even fairly liberal estimation of the size of these congregations cannot have made them more than about 5 per cent of the total population (Bogue and Bennett, 1808–12, III, 330). These figures are, of course, subject to a fairly wide margin of error, but it is hardly possible for the margin of error to account for the whole of the very great disparity.

Accepting the possibility that the increased flow of entrepreneurs in the Industrial Revolution may have sprung largely from Dissenting sources, and noting that these sources first began to establish themselves effectively on the historical scene in the century preceding the Industrial Revolution, historians have explored a range of possible explanations of the correlation between Dissent and entrepreneurial activity in eighteenth-century Britain. Since these have an obvious bearing on the study of the origins of the Industrial Revolution, they must be reviewed briefly here.

The traditional approach to this linkage has been through the particular characteristics of Dissenting doctrines. So far as the English Puritans of the seventeenth century were concerned, the doctrinal precepts which were particularly favourable to capitalist enterprise were the following:

In their emphasis on the moral duty of untiring activity, on work as an end in itself, on the evils of luxury and extravagance, on foresight and thrift, on moderation and self-discipline and rational calculation, they had created an ideal of Christian conduct, which canonized as an ethical principle the efficiency which economic theorists were preaching as a specific for social disorders. It was as captivating as it was novel. . . .

The idea of economic progress as an end to be consciously sought, while ever receding, had been unfamiliar to most earlier generations of Englishmen, in which the theme of moralists had been the danger of unbridled cupidity, and the main aim of public policy had been the stability of traditional relationships. It found a new sanction in the identification of labour and enterprise with the service of God. The magnificent energy which changed in a century the face of material civilization was to draw nourishment from that temper. The worship of production and ever greater production – the slavish drudgery of the millionaire and his unhappy servants – was to be hallowed by the precepts of the same compelling creed. (Tawney, 1926, 248–9)

Another, broader approach fastened on the contrast which the new individualism of Protestantism offered to the authoritarianism of the Catholic church:

In the last resort [Hill has argued recently in relation to the Lutheran doctrine of 'justification by faith'] conscience is the supreme court. . . . The appeal to inner conviction, and the rejection of the routine of ceremonies through which the priesthood imposed its authority, could have liberating effects in any society. . . . Since opposition to the Roman Church in 16th and 17th century Europe drew its main strength from the big cities, protestantism could be developed in ways which favoured the rise of capitalism. (Hill, 1961, 25, 35-6)

But if there was such an intensification of the capitalist spirit in the seventeenth century, it was not due, according to Robertson, who took up the debate where Tawney had left it off, to new strains of Puritan thought, but to a natural evolution of the attitudes of the capitalist middle class which influenced Protestant dogma, rather than were influenced by it:

The Protestant Ethic changed as a result of the influence of a rising capitalistically-minded middle class. The Churches of the Calvinists and the Puritans did not always bear the same witness as regards the duties of the man of business. A changing emphasis, reflecting a changing spirit of the age, transformed a doctrine outwardly uniform. From being a hindrance to enterprise it became a spur. (Robertson, 1933, 32)

Some apparent contradictions in this type of argument have been explored more recently by a Swedish scholar, Kurt Samuelsson. He stressed the extremely cautious approach to money-making of the Protestant sects in the seventeenth and eighteenth centuries.

In their general attitude to economic problems, the great Puritan teachers, with their mistrust of riches and the temptations of this world, were anything but capitalistically inclined.

He agreed that 'Puritanism unquestionably encouraged diligence and thrift', but insisted that this was only 'in the sense of low standards of consumption among individuals'. Nor would he allow that thrift, in this sense, was really what mattered when it came to the amassing of capital.

It needs no very advanced mathematics to demonstrate that thrift cannot have been the explanation of the wealth of such as Carnegie or Rockefeller. . . . Genius, sheer luck, a clear eye for market opportunities, a flair for publicity, hard work, low cunning, vast capital gains on natural assets – all these are possible and plausible factors. But to speak of thrift as a decisive or even substantial factor where large fortunes are concerned is utter nonsense. (Samuelsson, 1961, 79, 85–6)

Chronologically, the doctrinal changes in Protestantism which have been associated with the development of capitalist forms of enterprise were spread over a very long period. Even if, in spite of Samuelsson's vigorous rebuttal, Puritan dogma nurtured capitalist tendencies, the rise of Protestantism, Puritanism and Dissent in post-Reformation Britain can obviously be associated in only the very broadest of terms with an acceleration in the rate of economic growth beginning in the late eighteenth century. Ashton, however, has suggested another link between Dissent and industrial growth which is at once more practical and chronologically relevant. A unique feature of Dissenting society, in Ashton's view, was the role it accorded to education. On the one hand there was 'the stream of energy that poured into England from Presbyterian Scotland after (though not immediately after) the Union of

1707': on the other hand there were the Dissenting Academies of eighteenth-century England, 'nurseries of scientific thought' (Ashton, 1948, 19, 20). Many of the greatest industrialists of the Industrial Revolution – John Roebuck, Matthew Boulton, John Wilkinson and Benjamin Gott – were nurtured on the broad-based curricula of these miniature universities.

The Dissenting Academies were sufficiently numerous, and their curricula sufficiently industrially orientated, for their appearance on the scene in time to educate the generations coming to maturity in the mid-eighteenth century to constitute an important, and possibly decisive new element in eighteenth-century society. Yet, close on Ashton's heels, a work by an educational historian (Hans, 1951) has shown that the extent to which the Dissenting Academies were both innovatory and unique can be exaggerated. Hans has placed these academies firmly in the background of general advances in secondary and higher education in England in the late seventeenth and eighteenth centuries. What was new in this period, it appears, was not so much the Dissenting Academies in particular, as a broader academical movement, for the type of education commonly associated with the Dissenting Academies was also simultaneously being made available in academies run by and for members of the established church. Nor, according to Hans, were the ancient English universities quite as negligent in the eighteenth century with regard to the study of science as they are commonly reputed to have been. These wholly Anglican institutions did, in fact, play a not unimportant part in the dissemination of scientific knowledge. This in no way denies the significance of the Dissenting contribution to the development of forms of education more closely related to the needs of an industrializing society; but it does play down the uniqueness of the Dissenting contribution. If education played a part in paving the way for the Industrial Revolution, what was involved was a broader movement covering the whole sectarian front, possibly more intensive in the Dissenting sector, but by no means monopolized there. If this is the case, then the educational developments as a factor in the breeding of entrepreneurs and technologists cannot be explained wholly, or even largely, in terms of the rise of Dissent.

Sooner or later, most of the arguments relating religious with economic changes lead, in this way, into broader social issues. The most recent extensions of this type of invocation of non-economic elements in the study of economic growth have brought psychological techniques to bear on the problem. These approaches are still very much in their infancy, and their conclusions, though boldly enough asserted by their proponents at the moment, will no doubt go through a process of refutation, refinement and reformulation before they can take their place beside their more conventional economic companions in the analysis of economic growth. Two of these hypotheses, however, contain the seeds of what may be important ideas, and, since their authors have related them specifically to the British Industrial Revolution, ought to be considered here.

Both these approaches are concerned fundamentally with the increase in the proportionate number of effective innovators in a society. They recognize that the entrepreneur and the inventor have special characteristics of personality, and seek to uncover the process by which certain non-economic changes in society tend, through marginal changes in the social structure of personality, to increase the numbers of potential entrepreneurial and innovational types in the population.

Hagen (1964) sees the mechanism operating through the reaction of minority, or 'subordinate' groups to the 'withdrawal of status respect', by which he means 'the perception on the part of the members of some social group that their purposes and values in life are not respected by groups in the society whom they respect and whose esteem they value'. The withdrawal of status respect involves, primarily, 'the prohibition of some activity or relationship vital to the sense of status of a subordinate group, or a milder variant of the same type of relationship – manifestation of contempt, scorn, or some other degree of psychological ostracism by a high-prestige group of a subordinate group because of distaste for some element in the role of the subordinate group'.

The withdrawal of status respect is followed by two phases of reaction. The first is called 'retreatism', and was defined by Merton (1949), who first identified this social response, as 'the abandonment of both the cultural goals and institutionalized norms of behaviour'. Hagen's view is that, since personality, once formed, does not change easily, the reaction of authoritarian parents to the withdrawal of status respect will lead, in the first generation, to a change in parental behaviour which will shape a retreatist type of personality in the new generation. The son will discover that the father's norms and aspirations are unattainable, with the result that he comes to deny the importance of his father's traditional values, and to deny that 'he has any high expectation for satisfaction or contentment in life'.

But retreatism is not a dead end. It is merely a prelude to a new phase, which is thus seen as a natural, if indirect, consequence of the withdrawal of status respect. 'As retreatism deepens in successive generations, it creates circumstances of home life and social environment that are conducive to the development of innovational personality.' In this phase of the 'emergence of innovational creativity', change originates in the reaction of the mother to the weak, erratic, 'retreatist' behaviour of the father. The mother substitutes the son for the husband or her own father in her own pattern of values and aspirations, and requires from him 'the promise of achievement she sought in vain' in her father or husband. 'This sort of case,' says Hagen, 'is conducive to the sprouting early in life' of the personality traits of the inventor or entrepreneur.

Thus, a chronological social pattern has been enacted in which an appropriate personality structure has been instilled into a subordinate minority group. The prime mover was the act of withdrawal of status respect from that group, and the end product, after a lag, was the emergence of a small group with enhanced 'entrepreneurial' personalities. The point is not that this group has any monopoly of entrepreneurial ability – there are some individuals or groups in every society with this type of personality – but that an increment has been added to the proportion of individuals or groups in that society likely to make effective entrepreneurs or inventors. This incremental gain may turn out to be a decisive factor in raising the general level of entrepreneurial or innovational activity.

Two difficulties have been raised in connection with Hagen's suggestions. First, that they are largely hypothetical. Though they draw freely on psychoanalytic theory, they are assertive and lack the support of quantitative evidence. Second, and perhaps more serious, is their chronological vagueness. The duration of the 'retreatist' phase is nowhere made explicit, and though Hagen indicates that the subordinate groups he has in mind in connection with the British Industrial Revolution were the Dissenting sects after the Restoration, which would restrict the retreatist phase to not more than two generations, he inclines to set the phase against a much broader historical background drawing centuries rather than generations in its sweep.

The rival approach in this field contrives to avoid both these particular difficulties. It is the work of a Harvard psychologist, McClelland (1961). McClelland's approach sees human action – be it entrepreneurial, technological or any other sector of action – as resulting from the pursuit of the satisfaction of a range of psychological *needs*, and seeks to understand not so much the direction in which these needs are pursued, as the intensity or drive with which a chosen direction is followed. Since no personality is unique, individuals will vary in the structure of their need-patterns. More important, personality is both inborn and post-natally created. This means that one sector at least of the individual motivational pattern is subject to infantile and childhood (parental and environmental) influences.

There is, of course, a wide range of these needs, the amalgam of which determines individual motivation. They include a need for affiliation, which is a need for recognition, approval, friendship; a need for autonomy, to solve problems individually without outside guidance; a need to organize, to restore order out of chaos; and a need for achievement. Of these, it is the last which seems to have the most relevance for economic history, since McClelland is able to establish by a wealth of psychometric techniques that a high need for achievement is closely correlated with the principal 'entrepreneurial' personality characteristics, such as special attitudes towards risk-taking, willingness to expend energy, willingness to innovate and a readiness to make decisions and accept responsibility. McClelland demonstrates that there are wide variations in the strength of the need for achievement, not merely between different societies but also between different time periods of the same society, and between different individuals or groups of individuals in a single society at a given point in time.

McClelland devised means of measuring changes in societal levels of the need for achievement in the past, and established an index of variations in its level over the course of British history from the fifteenth century to the early nineteenth century, by which he claimed to show that major changes in the pace and direction of economic growth were anticipated at a distance of a generation or so by similar changes in the level of the need for achievement. His index, for example, takes a clear and decisive upturn at the beginning of the eighteenth century – at the moment in time, that is to say, most nicely calculated to prepare the ground for a major spurt in economic growth in the second half of the century. It only remained for him to explain how such a major shift in the general societal level of need for achievement was induced.

Personality, it is argued, is largely, though not wholly, determined in infancy and childhood, and the influences which operate most effectively on the level of need for achievement seem to be those which are brought to bear on children between the ages of four and ten. There

are wide variations between different cultural, social and religious back-
grounds in the attitudes of parents to child-rearing, and the condition
that McClelland found was optimal for maximizing need for achievement was one of conscious training for self-reliance and mastery which
kept clear of the extremes of leaving the child to make its own way
(arising from sheer neglect or indifference), on the one hand, and exces-
sive restrictiveness and authoritarianism, on the other. McClelland
believed that this particular attitude to child-rearing was to be found
during the Methodist revival of the mid-eighteenth century: 'the
Methodists' uncompromising stress on excellence seems almost certain
to have acted to promote the development of achievement motivation
in Methodist children'.

It is at this point that McClelland appears most certainly to go off the
rails. Methodism only effectively took root in the middle decades of the
eighteenth century, forty or fifty years after the upturn in McClelland's
index of need for achievement. Moreover, everything about Methodist
attitudes to child-rearing in the eighteenth century indicates that it was
of a most extreme authoritarian nature calculated, according to McClelland's own criteria, to reduce rather than maximize need for achievement. It is thus possibly no coincidence that Hagen's list of ninety-two
successful entrepreneurs of the Industrial Revolution (see p. 82 above)
includes only two known Methodists. On the other hand, there is some
evidence that the Quakers, the Congregationalists and the Unitarians
did advocate systems of child-rearing which correspond remarkably
closely with McClelland's requirements for maximizing need for
achievement: and these sects, numerically a very small section of the
population, produced an enormously disproportionate share of the
entrepreneurs and innovators of the Industrial Revolution.

There may, therefore, be grounds for extending Ashton's emphasis
on Dissenting education to include Dissenting attitudes to child-rearing.
Clearly, much work remains to be done to establish whether or not there
was a significant revolution to the approaches to child-rearing in the
late seventeenth and early eighteenth century which would have
affected the whole spectrum from infancy to secondary school age. The
evidence seems to be strongest in the case of the Congregational community, and it was this dissenting group which grew most vigorously
during the eighteenth century. And if, in fact, personality is largely
moulded in infancy and childhood, the generations of entrepreneurs
and inventors coming to maturity in the second half of the eighteenth
century may conceivably have been bred and increased as a consequence

of the distinctive influence of a dissenting upbringing earlier in the century.

The theoretical study of economic development has seldom proceeded far before it has been discovered that however the changes are rung on the strictly economic variables, they can never quite be made to add up to a convincing explanation of the initiation or acceleration of economic growth. While some theorists have been content to treat non-economic factors as parameters in models which study the interaction of the purely economic variables, others have expressed a wish to take the non-economic variables into account. Their desire has, however, invariably been frustrated by the apparent impossibility of quantifying variables in this field. Nonetheless, the non-economic factors continue stubbornly and vigorously to assert their existence, and difficulties of assessment are no reason for omitting them from an analysis of the Industrial Revolution.

> The economist approaches [this subject] with hesitation on more than one score. The disciplines to which it refers seem to him, in comparison with his own, undisciplined. To the extent that he can comprehend the jargon of social psychology, social anthropology, and sociology, their theorems seem to him either wildly over-generalized or self-evident. He is distressed by the fact that quantification is impossible. . . . It cannot be helped, for the matter is important. It is entirely possible – many people think likely – that the economic growth of France and Britain has been determined by traits of individual character and social process, rather than by geography, demography, finance, and such. (Kindleberger, 1964, 88)

VI
Conclusion

The industrial revolutions that are currently taking place in the mid-twentieth century enjoy at least three advantages: they are commonly supported by all-out government policies intended (if not always wisely directed) to induce rapid growth; they are normally able to import substantial sums of capital; and they can draw fairly freely on the accumulated technical experience of the rest of the world. Britain in the eighteenth century scarcely enjoyed any of these advantages. There was, as we have seen, a small net loss of capital overseas at the crucial period of acceleration, while the new industrial techniques adopted in the eighteenth century were almost all of native, not imported origin. On the other hand, as some of the opinions reviewed in the first chapter showed, there is a school of thought which associates the Industrial Revolution with a new-found freedom of economic action brought about by the abandonment of 'mercantilism' in favour of *laissez-faire*.

Since this book is not concerned with the means by which rapid industrial growth, once achieved, was sustained, the chronology of switches in policy must be set against the period of the initiation of faster growth in the late eighteenth century. Adam Smith's recommendation that the state should step aside in order that 'the wealth of nations' might be maximized through the collective efforts of individuals each pursuing their own best interests was calculated to foster economic development through increases in the division of labour. But though the *Wealth of Nations* was published in 1776, its recommendations were not immediately translated into government action. Nor, indeed, were Adam Smith's ideas quite so rigorously opposed to state action in social and economic affairs as is often assumed (Robbins, 1952, 37–8, 58–9, 115–17). Apart from some rationalization of import duties under the younger Pitt in the 1780s, and some modifications to the details of the navigation system and colonial regulation made necessary by the loss of the American colonies, there was no serious abandonment of the policy normally referred to as 'mercantilist' until the second decade of the nineteenth century, and even thereafter the change was gradual.

More important than the chronology of changes in policy, however, in the context of economic growth in the eighteenth century, was the actual impact of existing 'mercantilist' policy on industrial development in Adam Smith's day. For there are a great many respects in which a policy of *laissez-faire* may be said already to be operating long before Adam Smith wrote. So far as industrial development is concerned, that is to say, the degree of effective government intervention is easily exaggerated. Already by the early eighteenth century virtually all the elaborate and extensive provisions of the Statute of Artificers of 1563, concerning the training of skilled labour, the mobility of labour and the regulation of wages, were completely ignored. The gilds were virtually dead, and with them the power of the boroughs to interfere effectively with the course of economic development. The East India Company alone of the great trading companies effectively retained its trading monopoly. (The Hudson's Bay Company was an unimportant exception to this statement.) Industrial monopolies, whether chartered or patented, were things of the past. The many attempts, made over a long period, artificially to foster the growth of the woollen cloth industry were virtually all dead letters. The Union of 1707 had destroyed the last major internal commercial barrier, and the absence of internal tariff barriers gave Britain a very real advantage over rival Continental economies less favourably placed in this respect. Many of the new regulations which continued to be passed in the eighteenth century, such as the prohibition of the emigration of skilled artisans and the export of machinery, were extremely ill-enforced. The greater body of effective regulation concerned foreign trade and colonial development. While some of these regulations certainly hindered economic growth, others – import duties, for example – were primarily fiscal in intent, and taxation is a necessary evil afflicting mercantilist and *laissez-faire* ages alike. Alternatively, even Adam Smith was constrained to admit that the navigation laws were, on the whole, commercially beneficial as well as being strategically desirable, while there is little doubt that government intervention made a significant contribution to the expansion of the Scottish linen industry in the eighteenth century. On the other hand, in the field of banking, where government intervention in the shape of the grant of a monopoly of joint-stock banking to the Bank of England was a real barrier to the development of sound commercial banking, a mercantilist type of policy may be said to have raised a real hindrance to development. Similarly, the tariff and other forms of the regulation of trade were employed, as Adam Smith demonstrated, intentionally to distort the 'natural' structure of industry, fostering some industries which, without this form of protection, could not have withstood foreign competition, and discouraging others because they threatened the woollen industry. The Law of Settlement may have affected the mobility of labour, but recent research has shown how minimal this hindrance really was (Styles, 1963). The ban on joint-stock enterprise imposed by the so-called Bubble Act of 1720 did not apply to undertakings such as turnpike trusts, river navigation, canal and tramway companies authorized by Parliament, and on account of the relatively low requirements of fixed capital, was largely irrelevant to industrial organization in the eighteenth century. But the sum total of government interference with the course of industrial development in Adam Smith's day was slight, and by no means all of this regulation was necessarily prejudicial to industrial expansion. In contrast, the nineteenth century, with factory acts, anti-pollution legislation, income tax and heavier rating to meet expanding local government services, might even be said to have brought the world of industry much more effectively up against the realities of government intervention.

Thus, while it is patently an error of chronology to link the early stages of the Industrial Revolution with the coming of *laissez-faire*, there is much truth in the assertion that British industry developed in the eighteenth century in an environment relatively free from governmental regulation. Certainly there was no material *change* in effective policy which could have had any bearing on the pace of economic growth before the early nineteenth century. But there can be little doubt that the freedom of British industry, compared with, say, French, German, Swedish or (up to 1775) American industry, was an advantage favourable to economic development, providing other factors were also present to initiate growth.

The purpose of the four preceding chapters has been to argue that these other factors were numerous. The process of growth is complex, and any attempt to explain an industrial revolution in terms of a single prime mover is bound to be misleading. Inevitably a wide range of factors is involved, and each of these factors has its own chronology. Thus, the chronology of an industrial revolution is the sum of a large number of contributory chronologies. Since very few of the component variables can be stated in quantitative terms, the explanatory model cannot, inevitably, be assembled with anything approaching the degree of precision required by present-day theorists of economic

growth. Nonetheless, these manifold changes did occur in the eighteenth century, and the fusion of the many separate movements in the
right order transformed the economy and society. For ease of analysis
some of the component changes have been abstracted from the general
body of social and economic development and examined separately in
the previous chapters. Now it is time to reassemble the model, piece
by piece, and, if possible, in the right order.

In the process of reconstruction, two aspects of the problem must
continually be borne in mind. First, as research since Mantoux has
indicated, the Industrial Revolution was fundamentally a two-phase
operation: the period of rapid change in the last two or three decades
of the century was preceded by a long period of moderate growth.
Many of the factors discussed in the preceding chapters were aspects
or products of this moderate growth. But moderate growth tends not
to be self-sustaining either, according to Rostow's analysis, because of
its inability to generate a sufficiently high rate of net investment, or
because it is too easily overtaken by a higher rate of population growth
set in motion by the economic expansion. And even if, in spite of these
difficulties, a moderate rate of economic growth is sustained for a long
period, there is nothing inherent in moderate growth necessarily conducive to eventual acceleration in the rate of growth. If, as was the case
in eighteenth-century Britain, an acceleration in the rate of growth
followed a period of moderate expansion, the factors which explained
the initial growth will probably not also explain the later acceleration;
for that, a separate further explanation is required.

The second reminder concerns the nature of the Industrial Revolution we are seeking to explain. A strictly statistical approach which
expresses the Industrial Revolution in terms of the rate of net investment
or the rate of growth of real income per head reveals only moderate
changes in these rates in the late eighteenth century; and although these
changes still pose problems for explanation, they are problems on a
modest scale involving gradual and undramatic acceleration. A social
approach, on the other hand, sees the Industrial Revolution as a process
by which the nature of society itself was subverted: a predominantly
rural way of life gave way to the urban concentration of population;
the employer–employee relationship became institutionalized on
entirely new lines; and the pattern of class divisions set in a new and
firmer mould. Large-scale organization, which had hitherto been an
exceptional, though not wholly unknown, feature of the industrial
scene, took a great leap forward primarily as the result of the adaptation

of both old and new machines to water and steam power. Thus, any comprehensive explanation of the Industrial Revolution must take account of the variety of ways in which both economy and society were transformed.

For the purposes of analysis, some classification of the many aspects of change must be attempted. Broadly speaking, three groups of elements will be distinguished in the causation of Britain's Industrial Revolution.

The first is the accumulation of a set of necessary prerequisites. No chronological pattern is necessary; all that is required is that these conditions should have come into existence by a given point in time. It matters not whether they were created a century or a day before the acceleration begins. They are probably rather broader than Rostow's pre-conditions, since they represent not so much the first steps towards rapid growth, as foundations on which rapid growth is subsequently built. They must therefore necessarily include improvement in agriculture, since a major feature of an industrial revolution is an increase in the proportion of the population earning livings in non-agricultural occupations. The population which remains on the land need not necessarily suffer actual reduction: the industrial and commercial population will probably be recruited from the natural increase. The process of agricultural improvement need not actually precede the growth of population and its partial transfer to non-agricultural occupations; but, since it cannot be delayed until after, and since agricultural development from its nature cannot be achieved overnight, certain essential preparations must be made in anticipation of the acceleration of industrialization. And the faster the rate of growth of population when the explosion comes, the greater the need for advance preparations in agriculture if the Malthusian barrier is not to be reached prematurely. In eighteenth-century Britain these preparations took the form of a steady increase in the production of grain throughout the century, made possible by bringing more land under arable cultivation and by improved rotations; a sharp increase in the sheep population, made possible by the introduction of root crops and the improvement of pastures; and the general intensification in all branches of farming made possible by enclosures. The increase in grain production was premature in relation to the internal demand of the economy, but the additional capacity was held in reserve and its product exported annually until required at home (a procedure facilitated by the corn bounties). The great burst of enclosures, in the event, coincided very closely with the industrial changes; but though the act of enclosure itself may be accomplished very quickly and easily, enclosure as a social process needs long preparation. The legal machinery of enclosure must be formalized, and society conditioned to the acceptance of the social and economic upheavals involved. Both these processes may be said to have been at work throughout the first three-quarters of the eighteenth century.

There are ways, as we have seen earlier, in which the expansion of agriculture in the period preceding the rapid industrial developments could contribute to that industrial growth. But it must remain extremely doubtful whether the agricultural developments themselves would be sufficient to have played more than a modest part in stimulating an industrial revolution. For Britain in the eighteenth century, at best, they contributed to the maintenance of the moderate growth that characterized the first three-quarters of the century. But they were, at the same time, one of the essential prerequisites of the acceleration when it came towards the end of the century.

A second major field of change essential as a prerequisite to the Industrial Revolution was transport. Some of the transport developments of the eighteenth century were immediately connected with particular industrial undertakings and are best regarded as merely parts of integrated concerns. The greater proportion of the transport undertakings of the seventeenth and eighteenth century, however, being more speculative in nature, may be regarded as contributions to the growth of a general-purpose national transportation network.

The role of turnpike roads in economic development is often underestimated. Even quite heavy industrial traffic made regular use of the roads – Cumberland iron ore, for example, was carried overland on the last lap of its journey to the Vale Royal blast furnace in central Cheshire, while Newcastle steel for the Midlands metal-ware industry travelled by road from London to Birmingham – at 2s 6d a hundredweight, road transport added only about 5 per cent to the delivered price. Inland industrial towns such as Manchester, Birmingham, Sheffield and Leeds could hardly have existed without extensive use of roads for their industrial traffic. The movement for the improvement of roads by turnpiking began in the early years of the eighteenth century and reached its peak in the middle decades. The turnpiking of the network of main roads was virtually complete by 1760 (see, for example, the maps of Lancashire turnpikes in Moffit, 1926, 99; and of Nottinghamshire turnpikes in Chambers, 1957, 12), and in this way the development of turnpike roads was preparatory to subsequent industrial advance.

However, as industry expanded in the late eighteenth and nineteenth centuries, the increased scale of its transport requirements progressively reduced the utility of road transport. While the roads may have been a major channel for industrial traffic throughout much of the eighteenth century, the changing character of this traffic during the Industrial Revolution increased the importance of other forms of transportation.

These other forms of transportation all made use of water – coastal waters, rivers and canals. There were, of course, substantial improvements to harbours and rivers over a long period before the Industrial Revolution. In a small country like Britain, so well served with navigable rivers, there was little incentive or need to construct canals until the physical limit of the improvement of river navigation was reached. When canal construction began in the 1750s, it was, in most cases, initially a matter of extending the network of river navigations beyond the limits set by nature: the annual total of combined investment in river and canal navigation probably rose fairly steadily (short-run fluctuations apart) throughout the century until the 1790s, at which point further development was more in the nature of a response to the expansion of industrial and agricultural needs than a prerequisite. The greater part of this system of water transport – works like the deepening of the Clyde in the 1770s, the construction of the first major dock at Liverpool in 1709, and the extension of the navigation of the Aire to Leeds begun in 1699 – was completed before the coming of the major industrial changes.

Another essential prerequisite to rapid industrial growth is the evolution of a sophisticated monetary system – cheap and convenient access to commercial credit, a flexible and comprehensive range of paper money, and easy transfer of cash settlements both internally and externally. The chronology of the growth of these services was discussed in Chapter III, where attention was drawn to the view that some of these developments should be regarded as responses to rather than causes of economic growth. The monetary system at the time of the Industrial Revolution was obviously imperfect – witness the severe instability of the country banks in time of crisis and the drastic shortage of coins of low denomination; yet, thanks to the imaginative use of all forms of paper money and to the relatively smooth functioning of the sound cores to the banking system in London and Edinburgh, the shortcomings of the system were not vitiating. The paper circulation and the metropolitan banking systems were largely the product of the century after 1660.

Closely allied to these developments was the increased availability of capital in the eighteenth century, which was discussed in Chapter III. The act of investment, of course, is an integral part of the process of growth, but the accumulation of capital, which must precede it, is less directly associated with growth. While accumulation, in other words, must precede an expansion of industrial production, the expansion is not a necessary and inevitable consequence of the accumulation. Nor is a low rate of interest which encourages borrowing for fixed industrial assets necessarily followed by expansion. The increased availability of capital and the favourable rate of interest which fed it into industry may thus be more accurately regarded as no more than prerequisites of the economic expansion of the late eighteenth century.

A final prerequisite for major economic expansion was the provision of an educational system suitable for the new orientation of society. This involved the replacement of what was virtually a single scheme involving a traditional curriculum for a small aristocratic and middle-class elite by a dual provision which offered, on the one hand, a new curriculum far more relevant to commerce and industry for a new, broader, middle-class elite; and, on the other hand, an elementary education catering for the needs of a fairly substantial section of the working class. Both of these new forms of education appeared in Britain during the century before the Industrial Revolution. In England the academies, both Dissenting and Anglican, and in Scotland the universities, began to offer the middle classes, for the first time, an education more directly orientated to the needs of commerce and industry. At the same time the educational needs of the growing artisan class were met by the creation of the parish schools in Scotland after 1696, and the charity schools in England from the beginning of the eighteenth century.

Few of these developments in the fields of agriculture, transport, the capital market, banking and education would, of themselves, contribute much to the initiation of economic growth. Without them, however, the Industrial Revolution could scarcely have taken place, though their existence remained, of course, no guarantee of subsequent economic growth. They merely raised the economy to a higher level of probability of growth.

The second element in the initiation of the British Industrial Revolution was the emergence during the eighteenth century of a group of sectors of steady expansion. Expansion, in other words, need not necessarily have been general, but the growth in these sectors must have been sufficient to more than offset the stagnation in others. These sectoral advances were probably not chronologically steady, and the variations in their pace of growth – possibly cyclical – induced variations in the aggregate rate of growth of the national product. But at no time until the later eighteenth century was there a concurrence of significant shifts in production functions or of major changes in the forms of productive organization which produced a major discontinuity in economic development.

The sectors concerned were of two kinds – industrial and regional. Many industries were growing in the century before the Industrial Revolution, and in some – such as iron, fustian, worsted or some branches of the chemical industry – the rate of growth was sufficient to create bottlenecks and raise marginal costs. Where, often by chance, growing industries were concentrated geographically, as in the Derwent valley on the borders of Durham and Northumberland, the Stour valley in Worcestershire, the upper Trent valley or in London, the growth sectors assumed geographical form. In an economy in which industry was relatively thin on the ground, a quite modest growth in industries subject to some degree of geographical concentration was capable of producing sharp regional disparities in the degree and rate of industrialization.

The sectoral growth is important for a variety of reasons. Many of the elements in rapid economic expansion depend for their operation on the diffusion of a 'growth mentality' among businessmen, while so long as there is growth somewhere in the economy pressures are being set up which, on occasion, produce significant breakthroughs. These pressures may, as we have seen, operate in the technological field. With primitive manufacturing techniques and domestic forms of organization, for example, there are more likely to be diseconomies than economies of scale. These diseconomies certainly characterized domestic textile manufacture in the eighteenth century. So unproductive was labour in wool and cotton spinning, for example, that increased demand could only be met by recruiting domestic labour in villages ever more remote from the commercial centres, thus increasing transport costs and losses due to inadequate supervision. Similarly, so long as iron manufacture was tied to water power and charcoal as a fuel, increased output could only be achieved by wider geographical dispersion of the units of production. In this kind of situation, attempts to meet increased demand led inevitably to rising marginal costs, which in turn acted as stimuli to the discovery of techniques which would increase the productivity of labour or make use of new and more easily accessible raw materials. This process of technological changes was discussed more fully in Chapter V, and it is well at this point to recall the warning given there that it is one thing to set up pressures of this kind, and quite another to solve the problems they pose. The timing of the solution often had little direct connection even with the intensity of the pressure.

More particularly, the moderate expansion in these growing sectors is important as the source of some of the ingredients of the final stage of industrial revolution. For these sectors form the technological vanguard of advancing industry; they generate and train the new generations of skilled labour required to translate the inventions of the Industrial Revolution into practical commercial reality. It is from these sectors that many of the entrepreneurs and inventors of the Industrial Revolution must come: first generation entrepreneurs like Richard Arkwright were exceptional; more commonly, like John Wilkinson, Matthew Boulton or Sir Robert Peel, they were the second generation of a family which had already set its feet on the first rung of the ladder. Many of these second or later generation entrepreneurs built on foundations laid by their fathers, uncles and grandfathers. And with so high a proportion of industrial capital coming from ploughed-back profits, modest growth in one generation was an essential condition of faster growth in the next.

It is the existence of these growing sectors in the British economy ot the mid-eighteenth century that has led to the questioning of the whole concept of the Industrial Revolution. The notion that economic growth in the eighteenth and early nineteenth centuries was so gradual and persistent that the idea of a 'revolution' was inappropriate has been reinforced by the compilation of indices of aggregate growth like Hoffmann's index of industrial production (1955) and Miss Deane's collection of national income estimates (1955–56 and 1957). But there is often as much to be learnt from the disaggregation of global statistics as from their aggregation, while a purely quantitative approach which conceals qualitative developments such as changes in the organization of production or the acceleration of the process of urbanization misses important aspects of what constitutes the 'revolution'.

The two elements that have been discussed so far – the creation of a range of prerequisites and the superimposition on these of a degree of steady growth – do not add up to an industrial revolution. Nor do they in any way guarantee that the pace of growth will accelerate at some point in the future. It is the third element which is concerned with the timing of the beginning of rapid economic development. If a moderate rate of growth was a feature of most of the eighteenth century, then the explanation of the decisive change in that rate of growth that occurred in the last quarter of the century must lie in changes occurring or accumulating in the immediately preceding period. What changes were these? And how did they transform a moderate rate of growth into an industrial revolution?

The most probable pattern of population growth in the eighteenth century involves a significant upturn in the rate of growth of population in the middle decades of the century. The ways in which this population growth might stimulate economic development have been considered in some detail in Chapter II, and need not be repeated here. As was indicated in that chapter, the impetus to economic expansion arising from population growth is likely to spring from the cumulative effects of a wide range of mechanisms rather than from a single, dominating factor. What matters most, however, is the timing of the population explosion and the environment within which it took place. In many of the possible cultural and economic environments of a sharp increase in the rate of population growth, the only and inevitable consequence would be a progressive reduction in *per capita* incomes; but the preparatory and dynamic elements in the British economy of the second half of the eighteenth century were such that they not merely ensured that incomes did not fall, they also allowed the population growth to become a positive impetus to further economic expansion.

Population growth, however, from its nature, is gradual, and, while it may have contributed to the acceleration in the rate of growth in the later decades of the century, the precise timing of the 'take-off' must have been determined by other, sharper changes. These may well have been supplied in part by the changes in demand discussed in Chapter IV. The significant gains in the real wages of labourers came in the first half of the century, and though the general trend of real wages probably continued upwards until about 1780, it is unlikely that until then real wage advances did much more than sustain the moderate rate of growth. The more significant changes in demand in the last quarter of the century came from the substantial increase in middle- and upper-class incomes, and from the decisive rise in overseas demand after 1785. Though there is less statistical certainty about the first of these than there is concerning the second, both shifts of demand appear to have been significant and to have involved a proportion of the national income substantial enough to have had a real effect on aggregate growth.

There are grounds, therefore, for believing that population growth and the expansion of home and overseas markets may have contributed significantly to the upturn in the rate and nature of economic development in the last quarter of the eighteenth century. But, in the last resort, the decisive factor both in increasing the scale and in changing the methods and location of production was technology. The vast flood of cheap textiles, the coming of the new iron age, the summoning of the power of steam to the aid of industry, the aggregation of large numbers of workers in a single unit of industrial production as a commonplace rather than an exception, and the urban concentration of large-scale industry – all these facets of the Industrial Revolution stemmed from the adoption of new techniques of production.

The possible causes of the sharp increase in the annual rate of issue of patents have been discussed in Chapter V: there it was suggested that, while the progress of technique in individual industries might possibly be explained in terms of responses to the stimuli of earlier bottlenecks, the significant concurrence of technical progress in a group of major industries towards the end of the century may not be explained in these terms. It was suggested, further, that such a broad advance in the propensity to invent may possibly be satisfactorily explained only in terms of marginal changes in the social structure of personality. While the exact mechanism of this type of social change has not yet been worked out in convincing detail on the necessary interdisciplinary levels, the possibility of explaining the technological advances of the late eighteenth century in logically satisfying ways has at least been opened up. Social change of this kind does not, of course, occur overnight, and it would be absurd to suggest that the key inventions of the quarter-century after 1760 were the direct and immediate products of the socio-religious changes discussed in Chapter V. As an influence on the social structure of personality, Dissent operated continuously, and possibly cumulatively, from the late seventeenth century. The canalization of the growing streams of vigour into new innovational and entre-preneurial directions in the later eighteenth century may have been the product of wider economic and cultural developments. Shifts in the social structure of personality would, nevertheless, remain an important, and possibly decisive, dynamic element in eighteenth-century development.

Under the stimulus of buoyant markets, the new technologies shifted supply curves sharply. Reduced costs ramified throughout the industrial structure and new or improved products of one industry became the means of improving or reducing costs in another.

> The breakthrough in cotton textiles made it a leading or 'primary growth sector', as Rostow calls it, and the fact that it was accomplished by steam set up a chain of external economies in supplementary industries. The nature of these economies is of some interest. Most of them may have been vertical in nature, but the economy is not merely a sequence of stages running from primary to final products. There are circular flows as well – from ironmaking to steam engines to coal mining to iron making, etc. . . . In an input–output constellation of this kind, economies of scale will have a magnified impact, for the economies in one industry will return to it in the form of cheaper inputs. (Ohlin, 1959, 347–8)

It is, of course, one thing to initiate a take-off: it is another to sustain the new momentum. A further set of problems is involved here, but they clearly fall outside the scope of a book concerned with origins.

The conclusion to this study must therefore be the platitude that economic growth is a complex business. Because it is complex, it is necessary to take account of a wide range of factors. Each of these factors has its own unique chronology and significance; its significance varies with its chronology, and is, in turn, alternatively enhanced and diminished relatively as other factors rise or fall. The relevant factors, as we have seen, were social and cultural as well as economic and technological. This amalgam of changes amounted to a revolution in the last decades of the eighteenth century and early decades of the nineteenth century because many separate strands of development converged at roughly the same point in time. Disaggregated, the individual elements in the Industrial Revolution look gradual and undramatic enough; viewed as a whole, the process amounts to a sufficiently drastic upheaval to justify, in spite of the historians of the interwar years, the expression 'Industrial Revolution'. The ideal analysis would allot, as does modern growth analysis, a specific weighting to each of the elements, or at least would place the various factors in some order of relative importance. But eighteenth-century statistical data seldom if ever permit this degree of precision, and the best that can reasonably be attempted, it would seem, is some chronological arrangement of the various factors.

The three-tiered hypothesis which has been advanced in this chapter takes account of most of the factors which contributed to greater or lesser degree in the making and timing of the British Industrial Revolution. But because the three types of elements seem to have been present and to have interacted in this particularly dynamic way in eighteenth-century Britain there is no guarantee that a similar concurrence of events would produce a comparable result in another economy or another period. Only the totality of the historical environment can explain a particular course of events, and this totality, inevitably, is unique to this experience. This is, in other words, no theory: it is no more than a case study of economic growth. Theorizing is a form of abstraction which involves, as Domar has observed, 'snatching from the enormous and complex mass of facts called reality a few, simple, easily manageable key points which, when put together in some cunning way, become for certain purposes a substitute for reality itself'. The problem of the origins of the Industrial Revolution amply confirms Domar's belief in the complexity of economic reality. It would be unreasonable to expect this precise complexity to be duplicated elsewhere.

References

ABRAMOVITZ, M. (1956) 'Resource and output trends in the United States since 1870', *American Economic Review*, 46, Papers and Proceedings.

ASHLEY, W. (1914) *The Economic Organisation of England*. London, Longmans.

ASHTON, T. S. (1924) *Iron and Steel in the Industrial Revolution*. Manchester U.P.

ASHTON, T. S. (1948) *The Industrial Revolution, 1760–1830*. Oxford U.P.

ASHTON, T. S. (1955) *An Economic History of England: the 18th Century*. London, Methuen.

ASHTON, T. S. (1959) *Economic Fluctuations in England, 1700–1800*. Oxford U.P.

ASHTON, T. S. (1960) Introduction to E. B. Schumpeter, *English Overseas Trade Statistics, 1697–1808*. Oxford U.P.

ASHTON, T. S. and SYKES, J. (1929) *The Coal Industry of the Eighteenth Century*. Manchester U.P.

BAIROCH, P. (1963) *Révolution Industrielle et Sous-Développement*. Paris, S.E.D.E.S.

BARAN, P. A. and HOBSBAWM, E. J. (1961) 'The stages of economic growth', *Kyklos*, 14.

BEALES, H. L. (1928) *The Industrial Revolution, 1750–1850*. London, Longmans.

BEARD, C. (1901) *The Industrial Revolution*. London, Allen & Unwin.

BERRILL, K. E. (1960) 'International trade and the rate of economic growth', *Economic History Review*, 2nd ser., 12.

BOGUE, D. and BENNETT, J. (1808–12) *History of Dissenters*. London, 4 vols.

BOWDEN, W. (1925) *Industrial Society in England towards the End of the Eighteenth Century*. New York, The Macmillan Co.

BROWN, E. H. PHELPS and HOPKINS, S. V. (1956) 'Seven centuries of the prices of consumables, compared with builders' wage-rates', *Economica*, n.s., 23.

CAIRNCROSS, A. K. (1955) 'The place of capital in economic progress', in L. H. DUPRIEZ, ed., *Le Progrès Economique*. Louvain, Institut de Recherches Economiques et Sociales, 1955; reprinted in A. K.

CAIRNCROSS, *Factors in Economic Development*. London, Allen & Unwin, 1962.

CAIRNCROSS, A. K. (1961) 'The stages of economic growth', *Economic History Review*, 2nd ser., 13; reprinted in *Factors in Economic Development*.

CAMPBELL, R. H. (1964) 'An economic history of Scotland in the eighteenth century', *Scottish Journal of Political Economy*, 11.

CAMPBELL, R. H. (1965) *Scotland since 1707*. Oxford, Blackwell.

CHAMBERS, J. D. (1957) *The Vale of Trent, 1670–1800*. Supplement 3 to *Economic History Review*.

CLAPHAM, J. H. (1926–38) *An Economic History of Modern Britain*. Cambridge U.P. 3 vols.

CONNELL, K. H. (1951) 'Some unsettled problems in English and Irish population history, 1750–1845', *Irish Historical Studies*, 7.

COURT, W. H. B. (1938) *The Rise of the Midland Industries*. Oxford U.P.

CUNNINGHAM, W. (1882) *The Growth of English Industry and Commerce in Modern Times*. Cambridge U.P. 2 vols.

DAVIS, R. (1962) 'English foreign trade, 1700–1774', *Economic History Review*, 2nd ser., 15.

DEANE, P. (1955–56) 'The implications of early National Income estimates for the measurement of long-term economic growth in the United Kingdom', *Economic Development and Cultural Change*, 4.

DEANE, P. (1957) 'The Industrial Revolution and economic growth: the evidence of early British National Income estimates', *Economic Development and Cultural Change*, 5.

DEANE, P. and COLE, W. A. (1962) *British Economic Growth, 1688–1959*. Cambridge U.P.

DICKINSON, H. W. (1938) *A Short History of the Steam Engine*. Cambridge U.P.

DODD, A. H. (1933) *The Industrial Revolution in North Wales*. Cardiff, University of Wales Press.

DRAKE, M. (1963) 'Marriage and population growth in Ireland, 1750–1845', *Economic History Review*, 2nd ser., 16.

DUBOS, R. and DUBOS, J. (1953) *The White Plague*. London, Gollancz.

EPSTEIN, R. C. (1926) 'Industrial invention: heroic or systematic?', *Quarterly Journal of Economics*, 40.

EVERSLEY, D. E. C. (1959) *Social Theories of Fertility and the Malthusian Debate*, Oxford U.P.

GAYER, A. D., ROSTOW, W. W. and SCHWARTZ, A. J. (1953) *The*

Growth and Fluctuation of the British Economy, 1790–1850. Oxford U.P. 2 vols.

GILBOY, E. W. (1932) 'Demand as a factor in the Industrial Revolution', in *Facts and Factors in Economic History. Essays presented to E. F. Gay.* Harvard U.P.

GILBOY, E. W. (1934) *Wages in Eighteenth-century England.* Harvard U.P.

GILFILLAN, S. C. (1945) 'Invention as a factor in economic history', *Journal of Economic History*, 5, Supplement.

GLASS, D. V. (1949–50) 'Gregory King's estimate of the population of England and Wales, 1695', *Population Studies*, 3.

GONNER, E. C. K. (1912–13) 'The population of England in the eighteenth century', *Journal of the Royal Statistical Society*, 76.

GRIFFITH, G. T. (1926) *Population Problems of the Age of Malthus.* Cambridge U.P.

HABAKKUK, H. J. (1953) 'English population in the eighteenth century', *Economic History Review*, 2nd ser., 6.

HABAKKUK, H. J. (1955) 'The historical experience of the basic conditions of economic progress', in L. H. DUPRIEZ, ed., *Le Progrès Economique.* Louvain, Institut de Recherches Economiques et Sociales.

HABAKKUK, H. J. (1958, 1) 'The economic history of modern Britain', *Journal of Economic History*, 18.

HABAKKUK, H. J. (1958, 2) 'Population growth and economic development', in *Lectures on Economic Development.* Istanbul University.

HABAKKUK, H. J. (1963) 'Population problems and European economic development in the late eighteenth and nineteenth centuries', *American Economic Review*, 53, Papers and Proceedings.

HABAKKUK, H. J. and DEANE, P. (1963) 'The take-off in Britain', in W. W. ROSTOW, ed., *The Economics of Take-off into Sustained Growth.* London, Macmillan.

HAGEN, E. E. (1959) 'Population and economic growth', *American Economic Review*, 49.

HAGEN, E. E. (1964) *On the Theory of Social Change.* London, Tavistock.

HAMILTON, H. (1963) *An Economic History of Scotland in the Eighteenth Century.* Oxford U.P.

HAMMOND, J. L. and HAMMOND, B. (1912) *The Village Labourer, 1760–1832.* London, Longmans.

HAMMOND, J. L. and HAMMOND, B. (1918) *The Town Labourer, 1760–1832*. London, Longmans.

HAMMOND, J. L. and HAMMOND, B. (1919) *The Skilled Labourer, 1760–1832*. London, Longmans.

HANS, N. (1951) *New Trends in Education in the Eighteenth Century*. London, Routledge.

HEATON, H. (1920) *The Yorkshire Woollen and Worsted Industries*. Oxford U.P.

HEATON, H. (1932) 'Industrial Revolution', in *Encyclopedia of the Social Sciences*, vol. VIII. London, Macmillan.

HILL, C. (1961) 'Protestantism and the rise of capitalism', in F. J. FISHER, ed., *Essays in the Economic and Social History of Tudor and Stuart England*. Cambridge U.P.

HOFFMANN, W. G. (1955) *British Industry, 1700–1950*, trans. W. O. HENDERSON and W. H. CHALONER, Oxford, Blackwell.

HOLLINGSWORTH, T. H. (1965) *The Demography of the British Peerage*. Supplement to *Population Studies*, 18.

HUDSON, D. and LUCKHURST, K. W. (1954) *The Royal Society of Arts, 1754–1954*. London, Murray.

HUGHES, J. R. T. (1964) 'Measuring British economic growth', *Journal of Economic History*, 24.

JEWKES, J., SAWERS, D. and STILLERMAN, R. (1958) *The Sources of Invention*. London, Macmillan.

KINDLEBERGER, C. P. (1964) *Economic Growth in France and Britain, 1851–1950*. Harvard U.P.

KRAUSE, J. T. (1958) 'Changes in English fertility and mortality. 1781–1850', *Economic History Review*, 2nd ser., 11.

KRAUSE, J. T. (1959) 'Some neglected factors in the English industrial revolution', *Journal of Economic History*, 19.

MCCLELLAND, D. C. (1961) *The Achieving Society*. Princeton, New Jersey, Van Nostrand.

MCKEOWN, T. and BROWN, R. G. (1955) 'Medical evidence related to English population changes in the eighteenth century', *Population Studies*, 9.

MANLEY, G. (1952) *Climate and the British Scene*. London, Collins.

MANTOUX, P. (1906) *La Révolution Industrielle au XVIIIᵉ Siècle*. Paris, 1906; English edition (1928), trans. M. Vernon, *The Industrial Revolution in the Eighteenth Century*. London, Cape.

MERTON, R. K. (1949) *Social Theory and Social Structure*. Glencoe, Ill., Free Press of Glencoe.

MINGAY, G. E. (1963) *English Landed Society in the Eighteenth Century*. London, Routledge.

MITCHELL, B. R. and DEANE, P. (1962) *Abstract of British Historical Statistics*. Cambridge U.P.

MITCHISON, R. (1965) 'The movements of Scottish corn prices in the seventeenth and eighteenth centuries', *Economic History Review*, 2nd ser., 18.

MOFFIT, L. (1925) *England on the Eve of the Industrial Revolution*. London, King.

MUSSON, A. E. and ROBINSON, E. (1960) 'Science and industry in the late eighteenth century', *Economic History Review*, 2nd ser., 13.

NORTH, D. C. (1965) 'The state of economic history', *American Economic Review*, 55.

NURKSE, R. (1953) *Problems of Capital Formation in Underdeveloped Countries*. Oxford, Blackwell.

OGBURN, W. F. and THOMAS, D. (1922) 'Are inventions inevitable? A note on social evolution', *Political Science Quarterly*, 37.

OHLIN, G. (1959) 'Balanced economic growth in history', *American Economic Review*, 49, Papers and Proceedings.

POLLARD, S. (1958) 'Investment, Consumption and the Industrial Revolution', *Economic History Review*, 2nd ser., 11.

POLLARD, S. (1964) 'Fixed capital in the Industrial Revolution in Britain', *Journal of Economic History*, 24.

PRESSNELL, L. S. (1956) *Country Banking in the Industrial Revolution*. Oxford U.P.

PRESSNELL, L. S. (1960) 'The rate of interest in the eighteenth century', in L. S. PRESSNELL, ed., *Studies in the Industrial Revolution*, London, Athlone Press.

REDFORD, A. (1931) *The Economic History of England, 1760–1860*. London, Longmans.

ROBBINS, L. (1952) *The Theory of Economic Policy*. London, Macmillan.

ROBERTSON, H. M. (1933) *Aspects of the Rise of Economic Individualism*. Cambridge U.P.

ROGERS, J. E. THOROLD (1884) *Six Centuries of Work and Wages*. London, Sonnenschein.

ROSTOW, W. W. (1956) 'The take-off into self-sustained growth', *Economic Journal*, 66.

ROSTOW, W. W. (1960) *The Stages of Economic Growth*. Cambridge U.P.

ROSTOW, W. W. (1963) 'Leading sectors and the take-off', in W. W. ROSTOW, ed., *The Economics of Take-off into Sustained Growth.* London, Macmillan.

SAMUELSSON, K. (1961) *Religion and Economic Action*, trans. E. G. FRENCH. London, Heinemann.

SCHUMPETER, E. B. (1960) *English Overseas Trade Statistics, 1697–1808.* Oxford U.P.

SCHUMPETER, J. (1934) *The Theory of Economic Development.* Harvard U.P.

SMELSER, N. J. (1959) *Social Change in the Industrial Revolution.* London, Routledge.

STYLES, P. (1963) 'The evolution of the Law of Settlement', *University of Birmingham Historical Journal*, 9.

TAWNEY, R. H. (1926) *Religion and the Rise of Capitalism.* London, Murray.

TOYNBEE, A. (1884) *Lectures on the Industrial Revolution.* London, Rivington.

TUCKER, G. S. L. (1960) *Progress and Profits in British Economic Thought, 1650–1850.* Cambridge U.P.

TUCKER, G. S. L. (1963) 'English pre-industrial population trends', *Economic History Review*, 2nd ser., 16.

UNWIN, G. (1927) 'Some economic factors in general history', in R. H. TAWNEY, ed., *Studies in Economic History: the Collected Papers of George Unwin.* London, Macmillan.

USHER, A. P. (1954) *A History of Mechanical Inventions.* 2nd edn. Harvard U.P.

WADSWORTH, A. P. and MANN, J. DE L. (1931) *The Cotton Trade and Industrial Lancashire, 1600–1780.* Manchester U.P.

WEBER, M. (1904–5) *Die Protestantische Ethik und der 'Geist' des Kapitalismus.* Tübingen 1904–5; English edition, trans. T. PARSONS, foreword by R. H. TAWNEY, *The Protestant Ethic and the Spirit of Capitalism.* London, Allen & Unwin, 1930.

WILLIAMS, E. (1944) *Capitalism and Slavery.* London, Deutsch.

YOUNGSON, A. J. (1961) 'Alexander Webster and his "Account of the Number of People in Scotland in the Year 1755"', *Population Studies*, 15.

Index